THE GROUND AIN'T LEVELED NOWAY

A Play In Two Acts

A Play by Donyail Linsey

Dorrance Publishing Co
585 Alpha Drive
Suite 103
Pittsburgh, PA 15238
Visit our website at *www.dorrancebookstore.com*

ISBN: 979-8-8868-3020-0
eISBN: 979-8-8868-3885-5

THE GROUND AIN'T LEVELED NOWAY

A Play In Two Acts

Donyail Linsey is a young playwright from Houston, Texas. He has penned plays such as Black Crows, Spirits of The Mississippi River, and The Ground Ain't Leveled Noway. At Texas Southern University, He severed as, Professor of Technical Theatre as well as Director and Scenic Designer. Prof. Linsey received a B. A in Theatre and a Masters in Theatre.

This play is dedicated to: Jerry Lewis Jett Jr, Darrin Jett, and LaQuintia Sharda Lewis- Jackson

The action takes place inside a short order restaurant in Third Ward Houston, Texas. An old café it is, with a diminutive, aged steam bar. Behind the bar are swinging doors that lead to the kitchen. Left of the steam bar is a payphone attached with the message, "For paying customers only—Five minutes only." Neighboring the payphone is a restroom with a sign that reads, "Knock before you enter." In the center of the café, there are several small square tables with red-and-white checkerboard pliable covers. Right of the steam bar is a jukebox in desperate need of reconstruction. And it reads, "The Mudflat is not responsible for your money!" Customarily, stops are made at the pickup window where customers order food. The day is Monday, August 3, 1987, Sid's birthday.

CHARACTERS

Patsy... A woman in her mid-forties

Jabbo... A thirty-one-year-old inexplicable guy

Debra... A young waitress

Clancy... Owner of the restaurant

Jackmove... A man in his mid-thirties

Cadillac... A man in his late forties

Percy... A man in his early thirties

Monroe... A man in his mid-forties but looks much
           older (Clancy's best friend)

Job... A man in his late thirties

Janice... Clancy's sister (Young Doctor)

Sid... Clancy's older brother

ACT ONE
SCENE ONE

As the light comes up, Patsy is placing a variety of meats into the steam bar. She's a slightly overweight woman in her mid-forties and is sympathetic at heart. The clock has just reached a destination of 2:00 P.M. Patsy finishes at the steam bar and starts writing the day menu. Pork bones or beef tips, three sides, and a muffin for $4.19.

(Jabbo enters. He is a thirty-one-year-old man with a bizarre sense of amusement. Odd jobs are his employment, and business is getting slower)

JABBO

(Pointing at the glass of the steam bar) That one! I want that one right there. (Patsy is pointing at the wrong piece of meat, and Jabbo is getting more discomposed) Not that one Patsy! That one…yeah, that one.

PATSY

Okay, man, don't get edgy.

JABBO

(Takes the dish of meat, sits at the table, and devours it rapidly) Percy ain't been down here, huh?

PATSY

Naw, Percy ain't been here… and slow down 'fore you choke!
What you looking for Percy for anyhow?

JABBO

That nigga owes me some money. Why else would I be looking for him?

PATSY

Y'all need to stop fighting them chickens…Grown men, out
there making chicken fight to win money. (Walks into the
kitchen)

JABBO

Not no chickens! Roosters, women…roosters! Bring me one
of the rolls out of there too. What a black man look like trying to mistreat a chicken for? Niggas love chicken. The only
bad thing a nigga can do to a chicken is put him in a skillet.
Patsy why did the chicken cross the road …'Cause it was two
niggas behind him with a biscuit.

PATSY

Old joke! (Entering with two rolls in her hand and passes
them to Jabbo) Why y'all say that nigga word so much?
Every time y'all talk it's, "Nigga this and nigga that! There
goes my nigga! Nigga, you crazy! What nigga said that?" You
let one of the white men call y'all nigga, then you wanna be
a blackman… then try to jump on him.

JABBO

I ain't worrying 'bout no white man calling me a nigga. That's
what I am… a nigga! Some niggas don't wanna admit that
they a nigga… But me, I been a nigga so long I wanna be a

black man. You wanna hear my new song? It kinda sound like the Supremes. (He picks up the dish and pretends it's a microphone. Singing)

> "My nigga love
> My nigga love
> My nigga, oh, my nigga love
> You know them niggas treat me bad…"

PATSY

(Grabbing the dish from Jabbo) Man, will you give me this plate! (Takes the dish into the kitchen)

JABBO

(Singing)
"Don't take my nig away…"

(Exit the kitchen and cuts him off)

PATSY

Jab will you stop saying that word! Our black leaders have been fighting for well over four hundred years trying to stamp out that word, and y'all get 'round here adding a new definition to it… Calling each other that word ain't cool… It makes you sound like a dunce. You wanna use that kind of talk…go out there on Scott with the rest of the idiots… This here is a place of business.

JABBO

Ah, Pat, you know I don't mean nothing by that word. You the only one working today? Where Debra at…? She ain't coming in?

PATSY

(Yelling from the kitchen) She's on her way. (Coming out of the kitchen) I'm getting tired of this job! Clancy don't wanna give nobody no money… and I'm in here working my tail off.

JABBO

You could have six jobs, woman, and still couldn't work all that ass off.

PATSY

Okay, Jabbo.

JABBO

Woman, I'm just jiving with you. You sure are in a cranky mood. (Pause) You know how cheap Clancy is… Where he at anyhow?

PATSY

Him and Monroe went downtown.

JABBO

For what?

PATSY

To feed Sid…. You know today is his birthday.

JABBO

Why in the hell Clancy don't take that man from downtown? Sid downtown living like a hobo and Clancy got all that money. I would never do my brother like that. I don't care what kind of mental problem he has.

PATSY

You know how Sid act when he don't take his medication… Starts hitting all up on side stuff. Grabbing hold to stuff, like he gonna float away. Have folk scared to come in here!

JABBO

Ah, woman, don't nobody come in here anyway!

(Debra makes an entrance breathing heavily. She is a woman that works two jobs and is sometimes overhasty with her morning ablutions)

DEBRA

Sorry I'm late. Boy, I tell you these bus lines are something else. (She goes behind the steam bar wets a towel and wipes her face) Clancy isn't here, is he?

PATSY

Naw, him and Monroe gone downtown to feed Sid. Today is his birthday.

DEBRA

I see Sid all the time downtown by Woolworths… down there just staring at the sun. I'm surprised he hasn't gone blind, much as he looks at the sun. (Walking into the kitchen, raising her voice so she is heard. Clancy enters and takes a seat) Clancy with his cheap ass won't even put the man into a rest home…. Downtown living like a hobo. (Debra exits from the kitchen carrying a pie and is intrigued by Clancy's attendance. Clancy is a forty-three-year-old man, known by everyone to be a tightwad)

CLANCY

I'm a cheapskate, huh…? I'll show you a cheapskate come Friday!

JABBO

Look at you. You thought you saw a ghost.

DEBRA

(Placing the pie behind the counter) Clancy, you know I was just jiving.

CLANCY

(Goes behind the steam bar to check out the food) Debra, what time you get here? Pat, you better not lie for her either.

DEBRA

(Walking into the kitchen) I been here… what you mean?

CLANCY

See how Debra lies? Debra, I saw you getting on the bus downtown…. Pat, you was just fixing to lie for her too. (Pause) Oh, Jabbo, Percy told me to give this to you. (He takes out a ten-dollar bill and hands it to him)

JABBO

Ten dollars! What I'm gonna do with ten dollars? That nig… (Patsy gives him an evil look) sucker owes forty dollars. Hell, I got to pay my parole officer this week. Just you wait 'till I catch up with him…. That fool must think I'm Willie Fu-Fu.

(Goes over to the payphone to make a call)

PATSY
Clancy, how is Sid doing?

CLANCY
(Comes from behind the steam bar and takes a seat) The same…. I go downtown to take him something to eat…and he looked at me all crazy. Can't nobody talk to him but Monroe. We make it downtown…he down there holding onto the building. Like if he was to let go, he'd float away…like the ground trying to take him under… (To Debra) Debra, don't leave them dishes all stacked up like you done last night…. It's the man's birthday and he still doesn't know it.

JABBO
(Covering the phone receiver) Say, Clancy, keep it down over there. I'm talking to my parole officer.

CLANCY
(Looking at Jabbo very nonchalantly) Five Minutes, Jab.

PATSY
How old that make Sid?

CLANCY
Forty-nine.

PATSY
Sid ain't no forty-nine!

CLANCY
Sid is forty-nine…. Hell, I'm forty-three, Janice thirty-five, and L.B. would've been fifty-three last month.

PATSY

L.B. been dead that long? Yeah, that's 'bout right.

CLANCY

Hell, I know it is right. I know how old my own brother was. (Jabbo slams the phone down and stomps his feet) Fool, what's wrong with you?

JABBO

Man, my parole officer wants me to come to his office and take a piss test.

CLANCY

So, go take it. You haven't been doing any drugs.

PATSY

Yeah, but he's been down there with Percy them…. Down there on Tuam Street smoking weed, drinking, and making them chickens fight.

JABBO

Not no chickens… roosters, woman, roosters!

CLANCY

That's why Percy flagged me down to give me that money. Chicken…roosters…hens don't be, bring me into y'all crap.

JABBO

Ain't nobody putting you into nothing. That's all in your head. Let me get out of here, so I won't miss this fifty-two Scott…. What time is it, Clancy man?

CLANCY
It's 2:13.

JABBO
(Takes out a buck and gives it to Patsy) I'll catch y'all later on. (Exits)

CLANCY
What the hell he giving you money for?

PATSY
He had some pork bones 'fore come in here.

CLANCY
Plate of pork bones don't cost no dollar… Pat, I told you 'bout giving my food away. Next thing you know I'm gonna be feeding the whole Third Ward…then Fifth Ward gonna want the same.

PATSY
(Walking into the kitchen) Ah, man! Hush that up.

CLANCY
(Yelling out) And don't go in there messing with Debra…. Let her work. She late as it is.

(Jackmove bursts through the door. He's a thirty-two-year-old that is always looking to get his hustle on. Betting on sports is his job, and he can roll with the best)

JACKMOVE
Jackmove baby, who you thought it was?

CLANCY

I thought it was somebody with some sense…but it's just you.

JACKMOVE

Tonight is my lucky night!

CLANCY

Lucky night…? Lucky night for what?

JACKMOVE

The fight tonight…and I done put my last money on it.

CLANCY

Foreman sure do fight tonight. I'm gonna call Monroe up, see if he'll bring that big thirty-two-inch down here to-night.

JACKMOVE

Owee, Jackmove gone gonna watch the fight down at the Mudflat on the big color thirty-two-inch.

CLANCY

No Jackmove ain't! You ain't fixing to bring all them riffraffs down here with all that fuss.

(Debra enters with suds on her hands)

DEBRA

Jackmove, I thought that was you. When you get out?

(Jackmove tries to skip the subject)

JACKMOVE

Yeah, old Foreman gonna whip some ass tonight!

CLANCY

Get out of where? Boy, you done got yourself locked up again.

JACKMOVE

Man, I was on Mykawa Road. I just had a week in the P-farm.

CLANCY

For what?

(Debra takes a seat next to Jackmove and gives an ear)

JACKMOVE

Me and my lil' cousin, Eddie Combo… you might have heard of him. He plays varsity basketball for Phillis Wheatley High School. We was down there on Schweikhardt Street at this lil hole-in-the-wall ass club they call P&C. I was having a couple of drinks… and Eddie was on the other side of the club playing pool with one of his lil homeboys. Some guys walked in the club like they own the joint. I just stayed in the corner to myself…. I said to myself, "Just don't mess with me and my lil cousin." The guys headed right for Eddie. One fellow whispered something in his ear and him and those juveniles just walked right out the door. I go outside where they were…and they got this here, bag up to their nose…just passing it around. I took the bag from Eddie, and he just fell to the ground…must've been some kind of drug in there. I tried to wake him up, but nothing would help… Man, I… slapped him…I punched him…kicked 'em in the ass. Nothing would help. I looked up and them fellows were running down the street. I turn around, and this here police car done jumped the curb on me. The polices jump out of the car talking 'bout, "GET YOUR HANDS UP!" I thought to myself. "Get my hands up. I'm fixing to lay on the ground." They took me downtown to the Harris. County Jail…but I beat the charges. Thought I was getting out. The judge said, "Not so fast June Bradley… you got traffic warrants." They ship me over to the City Jail…locked me up and gave me a week in the P-farm. Felt like life in that hell hole…. Just wait 'til I get my hands on that Eddie.

DEBRA

Why you wanna sit up there and lie on that boy? You were down there with Jabbo them on Tuam Street…down there fighting them rooster in Peggy Scotchbottem's yard.

CLANCY

Boy, y'all gonna get enough going in that lady yard waging money on a rooster fight. Rooster ain't for fighting…rooster is for waking your black ass up in the morning…. (Gets up and heads for the kitchen) Fighting roosters…. Grown damn men out there making food fight and its people dying of hunger in Ethiopia.

(Enters the kitchen)

JACKMOVE

What Clancy talking 'bout Ethiopians for? He ain't gonna feed them. With his cheap ass!

DEBRA

I didn't mean to give you up like that in front of Clancy. But y'all need to stay away from that woman's yard. Clancy telling you right.

JACKMOVE

Damn Clancy with his cheap ass…. I'm a grown damn man. He always in somebody business. Ask him one thang 'bout Sid and he wanna jump on you. (Pause) Debra, you sure is looking pretty today.

DEBRA

June don't start with me. (Pause) You know…today is Sid's birthday.

JACKMOVE

Say what! I ought to ride downtown and see him…. You ought to ride down there with me after work… I'll come back by here and pick you up.

DEBRA

Don't make no sense to go down there. He ain't gonna say nothing to you…just look at you like you crazy and hold on to whatever is next to him.

JACKMOVE

Damn, Sid getting that bad in the mind?

DEBRA

Worse than that. The last time I saw him he was just gazing at the sun, without even blinking. I hate to see Sid like that.

JACKMOVE

Why Clancy can't get that man and put him in a home?

DEBRA

The same thang I said. But you know how stubborn that man is.

(Clancy walks in on the gossip)

CLANCY

Look here. How I take care of my brother is my business. And that's all I'm gonna say about that.

JACKMOVE

Clancy, downtown ain't no place for Sid to be living…. Got all kind of crazy folk down there.

CLANCY

Sid been living down there three years, and ain't nothing happen to 'em…. I can't risk the chances of putting that man in no rest home. Last time I had him in one of them homes…one of the aides put him in one of them glass elevators and he lost his mind… Medic told me he started taking off all his clothes. Talking 'bout, "The ground going under and I'm going over, but where them wings he promised…clothes you got to come off…got to make way for them big white wings." Medic said he like to had a fit when that elevator stopped. Told the aide he wasn't going anywhere 'til he, get them wings. Said if he leaves, somebody might get his wings.

JACKMOVE

Sid must have seen something in his past…Likely he had seen something in his mind that brought him to that state of mind.

DEBRA

Boy, that's some scary stuff…. I don't like talking 'bout spirits and ghosts and all.

CLANCY

Woman, it ain't no such thing of ghost. My grandpa told me that's just something white folk made up…. 'Cause back then black folk was really scary. He said back then black people feared their own shadow. He told me one time he used to work for this here white guy. Said one time he was up in the white guy's house, cleaning up his room. Said something came up to him in a white sheet talking 'bout, "Get out! Get out!" My grandpa said he went and got that rifle and said, "If you ain't dead, goddamn it, you fixing to be." Say that white man said, "It's me, fool!"

(They all laugh. Lights fall dark)

ACT ONE
SCENE TWO.

Lights come up in the restaurant later that day. Clancy is sitting at the table estimating the day's earnings. Debra is on the payphone, ten minutes to closing. A collision is heard at the front door, and Clancy walks over to see what caused the noise. He opens the door, and Cadillac's bicycle wheel plunges forward. Cadillac is a man in his late forties.

CADILLAC

Sorry, Clancy. Them kids running me down like I'm the popsicle man. (In a kid's voice) "Blow your horn, Cadillac. Turn the radio to another station, Cadillac. Go faster so that the backlight will come on Cadillac." All them fine cars out there…and they wanna scurry behind my bike. (Puts his bike on a kickstand and takes a seat)

CLANCY

You should be inspired. All them kids following you 'round like that. I can't even get them to buy a breadcrumb out of here. And you got them running behind you, like you Jesus of Nazareth.

CADILLAC

Man, them kids don't like me. They just wanna get next to that there bike… I tell you what… You ride the Cadillac, and I'll run the restaurant.

(Debra slams the phone down, runs into the kitchen, and comes out with her purse on her shoulder)

DEBRA

Hi, Cadillac. See you tomorrow, Clancy.

CLANCY

Debra, where you think you going?

DEBRA

It's quitting time… I got to go.

CLANCY

How you getting home? You need a ride?

DEBRA

Naw, Nemo gonna pick me up down by Wolf's Pawnshop.

CLANCY

You be careful down there…got all them smack and crack pushes down yonder.

CADILLAC

Be careful, Ms. Lady… (Staring at Debra as she walks out the door) "O, I could play the woman with mine eyes, and braggart with my tongue!"

CLANCY

Man, what in the hell you talking 'bout?

CADILLAC

That's from Shakespeare's *Macbeth*…. Damn, I miss the stage…. Hey, Clancy, fix me up some of your leftovers.

CLANCY

Man, you always come down here quitting time…talking 'bout leftovers. I don't leave nothing over. (Puts the money into his back pocket and goes over to the steam bar to fix Cadillac a doggy bag) I leave this food over for my baby Jesse.

CADILLAC

Man, is that old dog still living?

CLANCY

Sure is. That old dog heart is still pumping like an oil rig.

CADILLAC

I remember when I was a kid, I used to work for this here white man named Marshal Lee. I used to run with him doing odd jobs and whatnot. He had these four dogs. And everywhere we went, he used to call them dogs to go along…. Man, every time them dogs get in the truck, they started licking on me. I remember one time they started licking on me and I punch one of 'em in the mouth. Old Marshal Lee got mad at me. Talking 'bout, "Boy, don't be hitting my dogs like that. They just showing you they like you…. Look here. See how I let them just kiss me all in the mouth?" Man, I swear. That man was just sitting up there, just letting them dogs lick him all in the mouth. Used to let them eat off his burger and everythang. Man, I wouldn't love a dog that much. (Pause) Where did you get that old dog from anyhow?

CLANCY

Found him over there by Jack Yates. I come up on Sampson…. Little kids over there just throwing rocks at him. I got him. Put him in the car…and they started throwing rocks at the car. (Takes the food over to Cadillac and hands it to him) Here you go, Lac.... Yeah, man, I tell you them kids out there are something else.

CADILLAC

Thanks for the food, man. (Pause) Yeah, man, them kids out there is something, aren't they? Look here, man. I was down there at Flussie and 'em's house playing dominos. It was Flussie, Bay-Ray, Jamtoe, and me. We was sitting up there just playing dominos. The kids were out there in the yard playing. All but lil Fred...you know he's kinda slow and he always up under his mama. We were just playing dominos, and it was Jamtoe's time to play. But he wouldn't play. And I said, "Somebody please call 911, this man don't wanna play." Don't you know, Lil Fred went in the house and called 911. The police came out too...told us next time we call and don't need nothing, he taking the whole block to jail, children and all.

CLANCY

I bet y'all was scared when them laws pulled up... Man, these kids ain't nothing like we were back in the days. We didn't have all those games... We were out in the fields picking cotton. Boy, I used to hate picking cotton too. See, Dempsey, you don't know nothing 'bout that...you been living a somewhat good life all your days. But me, I was picking cotton. Every time folk cotton came in, I wanted to run away from home. While all the other kids were out having fun in the summer, I was going with my daddy to farm other folk land... . My daddy was a workaholic too. I'm talking 'bout a true peeler. I remember one time we were farming this here white man's land, and his crop was running out of time.... See, you had only so long to pick your cotton, and the government would make you stop. They called it underling your crop…. That meant putting your crop back underground. Man, I thought we was gonna have to underground that man cotton…. That white man said, "Damn the government! Y'all just keep picking." My daddy with his good hustling ass made us keep working. Man, I was mad…. Now the white man who we was picking the cotton for had his boy out there in the field watching us, like a lil slave driver. I can still see that boy's face…. Anyway, he had these grass snakes wrapped around his arms and his neck. Old Sid was hot, hungry, and mad. That white boy went over to where Sid was. Sid told him, "Boy, you best not come over here fooling with me with them snake." That white boy must didn't know how good Sid could fight. He said, "Shut up, boy! They just some lil grass snake." And tried to put them on, Sid. Man, Sid hit that boy three times in the face…. That white man came out there and picked up his son…. Man, I swear that boy looked like a devil and a unicorn. They run us clean out of Madisonville…. Been in Third Ward ever since. My daddy told Sid, "Since you hit so hard, you may as well get in the ring and get paid for it…. Took Sid up to that PABA, and Sid knocked everybody he ever fought out in the first or second round. They used to call Sid "Split a Wig Sid." George Foreman used to come up there. But he was too scared to get in the ring with Sid. Talking 'bout, "Sid too old, plus I'm a professional…. What would that look like, me fighting a amateur.?" He was just scared of Sid…. Man, my brother was cold with them hands. Would have gone pro hadn't my daddy and L.B. died.

(There is a knock on the door and in comes Percy. He is a peaceful man in his early thirties but often finds himself in annoyance because of the company he keeps)

PERCY

(Blows Cadillac's horn on his bicycle) Cadillac! What you say, Clancy?

CLANCY

Percy don't come here with all that fuss!

PERCY

Ah, man, I ain't causing no fuss…. You give Jabbo that issue?

CLANCY

Yeah, I gave it to him. He say that wasn't all of it too…said you owe him thirty more.

(Cadillac gets out of his seat, goes in the restroom, and Percy takes his place)

PERCY

Thirty more…. Man, Jab better step off that. I gave him what he won. He shouldn't have left the cockfight…. His rooster didn't kill the other rooster. His rooster just got him out of the circle. He don't win the whole pot. He must think his rooster Wizzie killed that man rooster…. He sits up there and take that rooster damn near everywhere he goes. Like that rooster is a dog or something. He a good fighting rooster and all… but it ain't like the rooster gonna make him a millionaire.

CLANCY

Man, y'all gonna get enough of going in that old lady yard, making them roosters fight…. Peggy with her old ass just sits on the porch and spits that chewing tobacco…and she gets a cut off all the fights. Just 'cause y'all in her yard, she gets some of the money…. Boy, y'all better wise up!

PERCY

Naw, she cut every other fight. Hell… sometimes she just be in the house watching wrestling…not evening worried 'bout the dead ring cockfights. (Gets up and goes over to the restroom and yells) Say, Cadillac, man, put some water with it.

(Cadillac comes out of the restroom zipping his pants up)

CADILLAC

(To Percy) The dead ring cockfight…. Y'all better stop fooling with Peggy Scotchbottem… And you better not be fooling with me while in the urinal. Boy, you're lucky I ain't got on a belt. 'Cause right about now, I'll tan your hind. (With a smile) Don't come fooling with me when I'm using the John.

PERCY

(To Cadillac) Look out, nigga. I'll knock you out like Foreman knocked that boy out tonight.

CLANCY

Damn it! I knew it was something I had to do.

CADILLAC

Do what?

CLANCY

Call Monroe, to tell him to bring his TV down here so we could watch the fight.

PERCY

Fight wasn't nothing but two rounds. That Fifth Ward ass nigga Foreman knock that boy out three times in the second round.

CADILLAC

Ah, that ain't nothing…. They got some cats turning pro that will beat the dog doo doo out of Foreman.

PERCY

Name one.

CADILLAC

I can't name one right off. They ain't come out yet. (Pause) Oh, I can name one. They got this here boy out of Catskill, New York, by the name of Mike Tyson…just wait 'til that boy come out. He gonna put some heads to bed.

CLANCY

Man can't nobody fool with Foreman but Ali…That's the only man who can beat him. You put anybody else in the ring, it doesn't even matter who…I done seen that young nigga Foreman beat a dude down in a telephone booth.

CADILLAC

Well, what happened to him in Zaire? I'm gonna tell the truth, I just don't like George Foreman.

CLANCY

Why? 'Cause the man from Fifth Ward?

CADILLAC

Man, 'cause he's a coward. Them promoters had to hunt this man down, trying to put millions into his pockets. Man, they tried to set up a fight worth four million five hundred thousand dollars to fight Ali…and he refused to sign with any promoter.

CLANCY

He still fought Ali.

CADILLAC

Yeah, 'cause Don King's slick ass conned him into doing it. He told Foreman so many people were out to sue him that not even if his lawyer Sargent Shriver got elected president of the US, all the Kennedys put together couldn't save him from bankruptcy. Don King told him, "Until he beat Muhammad Ali, the world would never recognize he was the champion." Told him, "As long as he keeps dodging Ali, he'd look like a wimp." (Pause) Foreman is the dumbest nigga I know. Let a gangster get right out of jail, and trick him into an ass beating. Howard Cosell talked 'bout Foreman bad too…. Now he's out there, trying to make up from where he done lost, and Ali done retired…. He should have never fought the man in the first place.

PERCY

Boy, that Don King is a slick one, ain't he? Quit Kent State College and started running numbers… went to jail 'cause a guy he had a fistfight with died…got out of jail, and now is one of the richest men in the world. If I was Foreman, I would've left Zaire. He saw how them damn Africans were cheering for Ali.

CLANCY

Well, y'all got a point there. Gorgeous George was kind of foolish. But I just like him 'cause he's a helluva fighter. Plus, he from Houston.

CADILLAC

I'm gonna tell you who was a good boxer. Sid was…. Man, Sid used to swing at fools down at the PABA and knock them out. Ask Foreman. He done had his share of knockdowns. (Pause) I remember I was attending Phillis Wheatley High School, and Sid was going to Jack Yates. I was never no fighter…. I was too wrapped up in Theatre Arts…. I was too pretty to fight. One day I was walking from class, I got into a scuffle with some guys in the hall…. They called themselves, "The Bloody Fifth Ward Hard Heads." Man, them cats could hit hard…and all of them were really tall, 'cause they were on the basketball team. But anyhow, I was walking down the hall, and the tallest one in the gang slap me across the head. Man, I called Sid the next day… Man, Sid came up there and whipped teachers, substitute teachers, jocks, cheerleaders, nerds, the assistant principal, three cooks, and a special ed student. And then jogged halfway back to Third Ward, 'til the fuzz caught him.

CLANCY
I sure do remember that. 'Cause I was going to Cullen.

PERCY
Say, Clancy, Sid used to box?

CLANCY
Yeah, Sid used to be a boxer. Would've turned pro if my dad hadn't died.

PERCY
I don't mean to get all in your business, but is that what made Sid that way?

CLANCY
What you talking 'bout, boxing or my daddy's death?

PERCY

Naw, I'm talking 'bout boxing. They say too much damage to the head can cause trauma.

CLANCY

Don't nobody know what brought Sid to that stage…. Sometimes I think maybe it's good for me not to even know.

CADILLAC

I would like to sit here and talk for a while. But the truth is, I don't want to…. (Laugh) Naw, I'm just kidding. (Grabs his food bag) I got to go by the junkyard…this here (Picks up his back tire) backend getting bad on me. And you know I ain't fixing to let nothing happen to the Cadillac. (Opens the door to leave) I'll catch y'all later. (Exits)

(There is a course of silence, and Percy calmly breaks the ice)

PERCY

So, Sid was a boxer, huh? I would've never known that. That explains why his hands look like big hams.

CLANCY

Yeah, man, Sid was something back in the day…. Today is his birthday. Man, I feel bad for him. I'm sitting here shooting the shit and my brother downtown plum out his mind.

PERCY

Why won't you get somebody to take care of him?

CLANCY

The only one who can sit and have a conversation with him is Monroe.

PERCY

Well, let him stay at Monroe's house…. Monroe got all them rooms.

CLANCY

Man, Monroe got a wife and kids and plus a brand new younger…. Monroe wouldn't mind doing it. But, man, I ain't gonna let Sid stay there with all them lil kids. I ain't fixing to put them kids in danger. I can see if Sid was just an old man. But, man, he is an old man that lost his mind.

PERCY

Well, he can't just keep living downtown. Something might happen to him.

CLANCY

(Puts down the towel, gets his keys out of his back pocket, and peeps into the kitchen) That girl done ran out of here and left them dishes piled up there again…. If you so worried 'bout Sid so much, go downtown, get him, and give him free room and board.

(Clancy turns the light off. They leave. Lights go down. End of scene)

ACT ONE
SCENE THREE

The next day. Lights come up on Patsy giving an order out at the pickup window. Jackmove is at the pay phone talking to his girlfriend. The time is 12:53 on a hot Houston Tuesday.

PATSY

(Handing napkins through the window) That'll be $4.19... Thank you, come again. Look, June, five minutes... Clancy come in and see you on that phone like that, he gonna bar you from coming in here. (Enters the kitchen)

JACKMOVE

Naw, baby, that's just this woman that cleans my house every Tuesday.... Something like that, but I wouldn't call her a maid.... Yeah, I got time. Where do you live? On Lockwood and Lyons...in Fifth Ward... You can't meet me nowhere else? (Pause) HELL NAW, I AIN'T SCARED! I just don't wanna be driving that far.... It's far to me.... Look, I'll call you back a lil later. (Hangs the phone up)

(Patsy comes out of the kitchen with a tray of food)

PATSY

Boy, you a scary man! Suppose to be a gambling man, but you scared to go to Fifth Ward.

JACKMOVE
Patsy, why you do that?

PATSY
(Putting the food on the steam bar) Do what?

JACKMOVE
Call me June, while I'm on the phone…. The name is Jack-move…Jackmove, baby, and don't you forget it.

PATSY
All right, I'm sorry, June.

JACKMOVE
See there. I thought I told you not to do
that.

PATSY
You said don't do it when you are on the phone.

(Debra enters, late as usual, and goes over by the steam bar to wipe her face)

DEBRA
(When she speaks, Patsy mimics her) Sorry I'm late. Boy, I tell you these bus lines are something else. Clancy isn't here, is he?

PATSY
Boy, I swear I go through the same thing every day.

(Debra exits into the kitchen, and Clancy enters. Debra exits from the kitchen carrying a pie. Clancy walks behind the steam bar to check out the food. He glances at Debra, and Patsy mocks him also)

CLANCY

Debra, what time you get here? Pat, you better not lie for her either.

DEBRA

I been here…. What you mean?

CLANCY

See how Debra lies? Debra, I saw you getting on the bus downtown…. Pat…

(Patsy cuts Clancy off)

PATSY

You was just fixing to lie for her too…. Damn, I swear I'm in the Twilight Zone! (Patsy slaps a towel on her shoulder, walks into the kitchen, and Debra accompanies her) Rod Sterling, are you back here?

JACKMOVE

What it be like, Clancy?

CLANCY

Hey, what's up, June?

JACKMOVE

(Leaving out the door) What is everybody calling me June for? The name is Jackmove…man, Jackmove.

(As Jackmove is leaving, Job enters. Job is a forty-two-year-old construction worker. Job takes a seat at the table)

CLANCY

What's wrong, Job man?

JOB

Twenty-one damn years, and now this!

(Patsy and Debra peek outside the door, and Clancy waves at them, giving them the signal to go back inside)

CLANCY

Say, man, what happened? You wanna talk about it?

JOB

(Stands up. Goes over to the phone, picks up the receiver, and slams it down. He walks back to his chair in tears) Why today! Why it couldn't be six years from now? All I needed was 'bout six more years. Vanessa starting college in the fall. Who gonna pay for it? The government…? Hell naw! (To himself, at a beat) Job Smith…you make too much money for Vanessa Smith to qualify for financial aid… Mr. Smith, you earn too much money for Vanessa to receive free lunch…will reduced lunch do? Every time I ask for something or need just a little help…it's always "you earn too much money…." Well, god-damn it, who in the hell gonna reimburse me for all the times I had to pay my own way? A man can't get nothing from this damn country unless you're down and out…. Make a little money so you can have your family living a lil bit above the poverty line, and what do they do? They penalize you for it. Well, damn it! I done had just about all the scolding I can take!

CLANCY

Job, man, when they let you go?

JOB

Right after lunch. My boss, Mr. Vandoff, called me off the overhead crane. I'm thinking he wanted me 'cause of some safety crap… I get in the office, "Have a seat, Mr. Smith." After twenty-one years, all of a sudden it's Mr. Smith…that's how I knew something was up. He gets me in his office, shuts the door, and said, "Mr. Smith, I have come to the conclusion that your service is no longer needed here at, Big Three." After twenty-one years of only missing two days due to the flu… After twenty-one years of putting up with all the racial slurs and unfairness… My service is no longer needed. (Pause)

CLANCY

They can't move you to another position? Got to be something else you can do up there…all them employees they have.

JOB

Man, I ask him that. He said, he'd call me if something comes up. I said, "Look here, man, I got an eighteen-year-old high school graduate daughter looking forward to her daddy sending her to college this fall…. It got to be something I could do in here. Man, I'll mop the whole steel mill with my tongue…just please don't put me on the unemployment line." He still talking 'bout if something comes up…he'd give me a call. My daddy was R-I-G-H-T on the nail. It don't matter how hard you work…it don't matter how dependable you are… Without your book learning, you ain't nothing but a drifting worker that's headed on the road to destruction… . But Vanessa is going to college. I don't give a damn if I have to wash every car in the state of Texas. My baby girl is going to college. (He gets up and storms out the door)

(Debra and Patsy return)

PATSY
Clancy, what's wrong with Job? Somebody die?

CLANCY
Naw, they laid him off today at his job.

DEBRA
Damn, that's awful. I mean, Job been on that job for well over twenty years. Damn, I feel sorry for him.

(Patsy and Debra walk back into the kitchen)

(Monroe enters. He is a man in his mid-forties with a sensitive and affectionate heart for his best friend Clancy)

MONROE
Hey, what you say, Clancy?

CLANCY
(Giving Monroe an amiable handshake) Man, I intended to call you yesterday…. See, would you bring your big floor-model TV? So, we could catch that Foreman fight.

MONROE
Man, I couldn't watch it my damn self…. Kids stayed up watching that *Brady Bunch* marathon… Then right after that my old lady took the notion to watch WKRP in Cincinnati. Left me babysitting.

(The order buzzer rings)

CLANCY

Pat…customer. It don't matter. Foreman won anyhow.

(Patsy returns from the kitchen and takes the order)

MONROE

Hey, Clancy, what's wrong with Job? Man, I tried to speak to him and he damn near cussed me out.

CLANCY

Man, Job just lost his job up there at Big Three Steel Mill. Man, I thought Job would retire from there… Twenty-one years he says. And they just up and laid him off.

PATSY

(Returning to the kitchen) Hey, Monroe…how's Linda and the kids?

MONROE

(To Patsy as she reenters the kitchen) They doing fine…. Yeah, man, I feel bad for Job. (Pause) You been downtown to feed Sid yet?

CLANCY

Yeah, I just not too long come from down there…He still down there holding onto stuff. I tried giving him his food. He started running from me. I chased him down, and the police thought I was trying to harm him. I said, "Excuse me, officer, he my brother…" Damn, that's humiliating. Sometimes, I think he know what he be doing.

MONROE
Yeah, Sid has more sense than you know…. Like the time I went down there to give him some roast Linda cooked. He looked at me and said, "Monroe, why you so nice to me? Everybody thinks I'm crazy but you…. You the only one I can talk to." He says people always say he's out my mind 'cause the way he acts… said he sees things that the physical eye can't see. Say he sees angels good and bad…said he wrestled with the same angel Jacob wrestled with. I asked him when did all this happen…. Clancy, who is the Gray done?

CLANCY
You mean the Gray Dog?

MONROE
That's what Sid was saying. The Gray Dog?

CLANCY
That's what my daddy called L.B…. Gray Dog.

MONROE
That's what Sid was screaming.

CLANCY
What was he saying?

MONROE
He just kept saying, "Get him off of you, Gray Dog…! Get him off of you!" And took off running down the block… People thought I did something to 'em.

CLANCY
That's why he always says, "Give me my wings. They prom-

ised me some wings." Sid thinking he done saw some angels.

MONROE
When he started losing his mind?

CLANCY
Right after my daddy died…. When L.B. died he got even worse…. You ain't notice how he started staying to himself.

MONROE
Why don't you take his next SSI check and take him to see a psychiatrist?

CLANCY
A psychiatrist can't do nothing for Sid. They ain't gonna do nothing but give him some medicine that will calm him down for a while. After that, he'll be in the worst state he was in before that.

MONROE
Clancy, you got to do something. He just can't say downtown forever…. You better get him 'fore he does something to somebody, or somebody do something to him.

CLANCY
I'm trying to get Janice over here. See if she can keep him awhile.

(Monroe stands up and walks over to the door, and Clancy follows)

MONROE
Man, if it's anything you need, day or night, just give me a call. (Shakes Clancy's hand and exits the door. The buzzer rings)

CLANCY
Debra! Patsy! Y'all got a customer out here!

(He sits at the table with a look of misfortune on his face. The lights fade to dark)

ACT ONE
SCENE FOUR

Lights come up on Debra taking an order two days later. Percy and Jabbo are at the table eating. They have just come back from a cockfight, and both were prosperous.

JABBO

Debra, bring me some more of that cornbread…. Like I was saying, man. You need to take care that 'fore it gets out of hand.

DEBRA

(Handing Jabbo a couple of cornbread muffins) 'Fore what gets out of hand?

JABBO

Woman mind your own! This here is man talk…. And what's up with you and that nigga Nemo? You know what he do for a living?

DEBRA

It ain't none of your business what he does for a living…. Like fighting rooster is an occupation.

JABBO

It's better than slang'n crack.

PERCY

Who you talking 'bout sell crack?

JABBO

Some jive-ass nigga she dealing with name Nemo. Drive that big green Mercury, with that big antenna on the back…. Riding by folk's house giving them free cable and shit…. Nigga's car so big and long, he got to have a CDL license to drive it.

DEBRA

Jabbo, if you gonna use that type of language, you gonna have to leave here.

PERCY

Come on, man, leave Debra alone…finish telling me what we need to do.

JABBO

We'll talk about it later.

(Janice makes an entrance. She's Clancy younger sister. Janice is a thirty-five-year-old doctor that has labored laboriously to get the position she's in. She walks in with a doctor uniform on and a briefcase)

JANICE

Hello, how are you all? Is Clancy in?

DEBRA

Naw, he's not in yet. Have a seat and wait for him…. Can I get you anything?

JANICE

(Taking a seat, Percy and Jabbo glare in lust) Some water, please.

(Debra walks into the kitchen to get the glass of water. Percy slides over to where Janice is sitting)

JABBO

(Giving Percy a handshake) Look here, man, I'll get up with you later on on that.

PERCY

All right, man. Take it easy…. I'll catch up with you by Peggy. (To Janice) How you doing, Ms. Lady?

JANICE

(Fumbling around in her briefcase) Fine, and yourself?

PERCY

I'm cool…. Say, what hospital you work at?

JANICE

St. Luke's.

(Debra brings Janice a glass of water and the buzzer rings. She goes over to answer it, and it's her boyfriend Nemo)

DEBRA

Nemo, what you doing here? You gonna live a long time…. Hold on. I'll be out there. (Takes her apron off and flings it onto the floor) Percy, if Clancy comes, tell him I'm right out here. (Exits)

PERCY

(To Debra) All right then…. (To Janice) St. Luke! I had a friend used to work up there…. She wasn't no nurse like you. She worked in the kitchen.

JANICE

I don't mean to be rude, but I'm not a nurse. I'm a doctor.

PERCY

I don't mean to be rude either. But doctor… nurse…surgeon, hell, it's all the same.

JANICE

It's different types for each one. Like, for instance, I'm an MD, Doctor of Medicine. And there are many types of MD. You have general practitioners, physicians, surgeons, chiropractors…and the list goes on.

PERCY

Well. What kind of MD are you?

JANICE

I'm what they call a pediatrician.

PERCY

I thought that meant a person…. You know if somebody is like, walking across the street. You always see those signs. They say, "Please watch for per…"

JANICE

No. You are talking about pedestrians…. No, I'm a pediatrician, a doctor that aids children.

PERCY

(A little embarrassed) Oh…Oh, that's nice.

JANICE

Do you have any kids… Ahh, I didn't get your name.

PERCY

(Extending his hand out) Percy… The name is Percy Lumpkin. Naw, I don't have any kids. I had a little girl at one time…but now she's gone.

JANICE

What happened to her? Did she die?

PERCY

Naw, her and her mama run off to Chicago 'bout six summers ago.

JANICE

Why did they leave?

PERCY

Well, see, I was working two jobs. One job in the morning, and one job at night. I would get home and she had nothing cooked. I would say, "Fay…" That was her name, Fay. I would say, "Fay, why you haven't cooked nothing?" She would look at me and say, "Why you didn't eat where you just come from?" I said, "Woman, I just came from work." She would take our child to the other room and just slam the door. Don't you know? I was out there working my ass off, and she thought I was cheating 'cause I wouldn't show her my check subs. So, one day I came home, and they were gone.

JANICE

Well, how do you know they moved to Chicago?

PERCY

When the government started making me pay her child support.

JANICE

Oh… What do you do for a living?

PERCY

I promote chickens and roosters.

JANICE

You promote chickens and roosters…? What, do they perform tricks or something?

PERCY

Yeah, they perform all right… They fight.

JANICE

What? You make them fight each other?

PERCY

Naw, they fight other roosters…. See, it's called cockfighting. You get you a rooster, lock 'em up for 'bout five days. Then you take 'em down to a cockfight. Now at a cockfight, you got to have yourself a bad rooster, if not you can lose all your money. You saw that fellow that just left out of here? Well, him and me fixing to buy this here piece of land lil bit past Dallas. Start raising the most fearless…the bravest animals. I'm talking 'bout fighting dogs, fighting roosters, wild fighting hogs, racing greyhounds, prize-winning pigs…. Jabbo is in it for the money, but for me, I just like the excitement of it.

JANICE

That's so unkind and hardhearted.

PERCY

I ain't in it for the money. I really love animals.

JANICE

Well, why do you make them fight if you love them so much?

PERCY

I don't know, I just do.

JANICE

Say, for instance, you obtain this portion of land. Where are you going to get the animals?

PERCY

Ah, animal ain't no problem to get. It's getting them trained to fight.

JANICE

I don't know. It just sounds like, an uncanny way of making a living…. I remember when I was a little girl, I had this little chick. I mean, I raised that thing from a chick to a chicken. I allow that chicken to sleep with me…even eat with me. See, my brothers used to go pick cotton with my daddy. And my mother and I would remain at home and take care of the house. One day it was really scorching hot, and Mother told me I could go and take a nap. So, I went into the living room. Made me a pallet on the floor by the air conditioner vent. I can still sense that frigid air hitting the top of my braids, freezing the trickling sweat in the parts on my head. Anyway, my brothers came home after an extensive day of picking… and they were mad. My oldest brother, God rest his soul, came into the house in anger…and flanged me off of my pallet. I storm into the room to tell my daddy. I said, "Daddy,

Gray Dog in there picking with me." That's what we called my brother L.B. "Gray Dog," I said, "Daddy, Gray Dog in there picking." My daddy didn't take any jive. When he said something, you did it or you get that strap put on your backside. My daddy said, "Gray Dog, don't have me to come in there with my strap…'cause if I come in there, I'm gonna blister your behind." I started laughing at him, and that made him angry. So, he went out on the porch, got his big hunting knife, and cut my chicken's head off. I heard something making a lot of noise. So, I ran outside to see what it was. And there my chicken was. Just running around in the yard without a head. I ran and got my daddy. Boy, you should have seen my daddy's face. He was mad as heck. He made my brother pick all the feathers out with his teeth and drink a cup of its blood. That made me feel a little bit better…but I was still upset.

PERCY
I would have killed your chicken too…. I'm coming home from picking cotton in the hot sun. And here you are lying up under the air conditioner. But I would have killed him and eaten him.

JANICE
(Hitting Percy on the hand) Oh, you would have killed my chicken?

PERCY
(Tapping her back) Sure would have.

(Janice notices the dirt under Percy's nails and grabs them for cleaning)

JANICE

I don't mean to be rude, but under your fingernails are filthy. Do you mind if I clean them for you?

PERCY

Naw! Clancy ain't fixing to come in here and catch us hand in hand.

JANICE

Percy, I'm a grown woman…. Besides, I'm just cleaning your nails.

PERCY

What if your man walks through the door?

JANICE

Percy, I… You're just trying to find out if I have a husband or not…and for your information, I do not. I don't have a boyfriend either…. I'm single.

PERCY

Well, can you mingle?

JANICE

I don't have time to mingle. I'm a doctor, remember?

PERCY

That don't mean you can't mingle…. Look here, let me pick you up one day.

JANICE

No, I don't think so. (Pause) Let me pick you up.

PERCY

Hot damn it! That's what I'm talking 'bout... an independent woman…. Janice, what type of car you driving?

JANICE

I don't mean to be a braggart, but I drive a Mercedes-Benz.

PERCY

You telling Percy you got yourself one of them foreign automobiles?

JANICE

Look outside and see.

PERCY

(He gets up and peeks out the door) Damn, that's a fine car… A fine car…for a fine woman.

JANICE

Percy, I'm a doctor. I don't collect cans.

PERCY

I know, but it's just so hard to believe that a woman can have all this by herself…. I'm talking 'bout a woman that can get up and go get anything she wants. All the women I done come in contact with are just trying to get into a man's pocket. But you…you don't need for nothing I bet…. Pay your own bills. Ain't got to stay home and clean the house… And try to clean it up extra good on a Friday so your man might feel sorry for you and give you a lil piece of his paycheck. I ain't saying that a woman shouldn't stay home and take care of her family. Money ain't everything. I'm just saying…you gonna set a trend for all the independent women to come…. A woman that can take charge of her own life. You know, set her own rules. (He stands up and dramatizes as if he is taking a picture of her) Just let me take a picture of you. (Janice blushes) I wanna take a picture of you…take it up to Kmart, and get it blown up. Have a lil marquee at the bottom with flashing colorful lights that read. CAREER WOMAN OF THE EIGHTIES. Might even make a movie out of it. "Working woman without a man's touch." Look at you blush…. You know you got it all.

JANICE

You think because I have a good job and a nice car, I'm happy? Not having a man is no walk in the park. Sometimes I get lonely. Having a big sum of money can't keep a woman or man warm at night when it's cold. When I was in medical school, I didn't want to look at a man. Because I was so focused on my main objective of becoming a doctor. I was so determined to become a doctor. I thought, "Who needs a man when you have such a promising career." Seventeen years of my life have passed, and I haven't had the chance to sit down and really enjoy it at all. Sure, I want to go to the movies or take a walk in the park. But I'm obligated to children now…and I just can't throw that away. My mother and father, God rest their souls, pushed me too hard to just give up now for a family…. It's just so much I must deal with right now. (At a beat) The death of my mother… The death of my father… The death of my brother… The insanity of my other brother Sid. (Breaking out in tears) It's just so much for one woman to deal with!

PERCY

Look here, Janice. I know I may not have a steady job or a fancy car. But there is something I got that you need, and that's love. It's like God made us meet here today. You are looking for a man to love… And I'm looking for a woman to help me find my niche in life. I can't help you pay your car note or give you money for your mortgage, but I can treat you like the queen you are. I'm talking about cooking for you…cleaning for you…bathing you, and in between all that. We'll make some beautiful children. Since you love kids so much, I'll give you children you can love even more…. I probably can't give you the finer things in life. But I guarantee I'll keep you happy from the going down of the sun… until the crowing of the rooster.

JANICE

That's easy to say. We just met. But what if I didn't have all this? Would you still want to be with me? (Pause) What I'm I talking about? I don't even know you.

PERCY

Let me tell you something, Janice…I ain't never owned a thing in my life. Even this body that sits before you don't belong to me. So material things don't mean a thing to me…. It's all about living your life…. Not about how much money you make or how many years you went to school. I drop out of school in the tenth grade. Not "cause I was dumb. Because it was meant to happen like that, and I couldn't stop that, as much as people couldn't stop you from becoming a doctor. It's just something you can't control…it's called fate. Hell, my dad never went to school a day in his life. But he mastered the most complicated subject ever taught… Life! He didn't have a big, fancy house or a big, sparkling diamond ring to put on my mom finger. But he did the little things, that so-called big people think are little…. Let me show you something. (He grabs her from behind and hugs her) How does that feel?

JANICE

It feels comfortable…loving…breathtaking…securing.

(Percy turns towards Janice, goes in his pocket, and hands her a ten-dollar bill)

PERCY

Now how does that feel?

JANICE

Feels like you just paid me for some sexual favor…like I'm a harlot or something.

PERCY

That goes to show you that love is more powerful than money.

(They gaze at each other. Moments later they kiss. Clancy and Debra walk in, astounded, and the lights fall black)

ACT ONE
SCENE FIVE

Days later, Clancy and Monroe are sitting at the table drinking coffee.

CLANCY

I walk in and there they were…kissing each other.

MONROE

Yeah, man, but Janice is a grown woman now… thirty-five years of age. She ain't no lil girl anymore…. You ain't that much older than her.

CLANCY

I know that, man! But my folks ain't push her through medical school so she could become a doctor, then go out with some thug. She's a doctor for God's sake…she deserves better.

MONROE

Ah, man, you just saying that 'cause she's your sister…. Being a doctor ain't got a thing to do with it. Percy ain't that bad of a fellow…. Now I could see if she was dating Jabbo… But Percy ain't that bad. He just gets mixed up with the wrong crowd.

CLANCY

Percy ain't no different from none of these hustling niggas…
I like Jabbo better than I like Percy…. See, Jab will tell you

when he fixing to do something.... He'll get right to the point. But for that nigga Percy, he'll sneak and do it, and deny it.... Monroe, will you just look at the big picture? He's just after Janice money.

MONROE

Why when a woman finds a man that makes a lot of money, they say she found a good man, but if a man finds a woman that makes a lot of money, he's trying to hustle her?

CLANCY

Monroe, Janice don't know nothing 'bout these here streets.... She sprouted up under my mama and daddy. Never wanted for nothing.... Hell, her belly was full when the whole family was hungry. My daddy worked damn near three jobs to make sure that girl would be the first to graduate from college.

MONROE

And she graduated from college.... Look, Clancy, you getting yourself all worked up for nothing. This lil friendship of theirs might blow off tomorrow.

CLANCY

Man, it's been damn near a week and they are still together... Parading my sister 'round town like she is the Queen Sheba. And she got her nose so open, she can smell a fart in China.

(Monroe laughs)

MONROE

Damn, man, you silly. Sitting up here, worrying 'bout a thirty-five-year-old woman.... Man, you ought to stop.

CLANCY

Monroe, I'm serious 'bout this…. This ain't no laughing matter. My brother is downtown out of his mind…and…she out there fooling around somewhere…. Probably ain't even been going to work. Walking 'round with a dude she don't know a damn thang about.

MONROE

Say, man, take your mind off that. Janice is a grown woman. She can fend for herself. (He gets up and goes over to the jukebox) Clancy, when are you gonna get this thing fixed?

CLANCY

(Gazing off into space) That thing has been broke since the day I bought it…. Bought it from a fellow named Gus…. He let me have it for forty bucks.

MONROE

Forty bucks! Damn, it don't take nothing but thirty to fix… You wanna sell it?

CLANCY

(Gets up and walks toward the kitchen) What in the hell are you gonna do with it, Monroe? What you thinking 'bout opening up a Juke Joint? (Walks into the kitchen and comes out with cream for his coffee)

MONROE

Hell naw! I figure I'd put it up in one of my rooms. Put me some old tunes in here. Might put me some B.B. King or some Muddy Waters in here… Boy, my daddy loved that boy Muddy Waters. Used to always sing, "Got My Mojo Working." I bet he still listening to Muddy Waters. Man, back then I couldn't stand the blues. But now that I'm much older, I can see where my old man was coming from. I'm gonna call my daddy up today and see if he still got Muddy's records.

CLANCY

Monroe, I know y'all people from Lafayette, but where are your folks living now?

MONROE

Down in Lake Charles. They still in Louisiana. They ain't going nowhere. Louisiana they were born…Louisiana they gonna die.

CLANCY

We got people up in Louisiana too… Last name Mamou.

MONROE

What part are they from?

CLANCY

St. Martinsville… My uncle owns a café down there called The Mudflats…. That's why I name my place The Mud-flats.

MONROE

The club still up?

CLANCY

 Naw, the no-good Klan burned it to ashes five years ago. Had the whole town mad…. White people and all. Down in St. Martinsville, everybody gets along…all neighborly like… Town don't allow no riffraff's.

MONROE

That's how you keep your town safe…. Keep all them riff-raff's out. My daddy is somewhat a riffraff… But he ain't the starting trouble type of riffraff. He's a joke-telling riff-raff. We ain't nothing alike, but we look alike. Man, my daddy can crack your side telling them jokes. Me and my cousins used to sneak and listen to him telling my uncle 'em jokes all the time. Man, I know 'bout a thousand and one damn jokes.

CLANCY

(Stirring his coffee) Well, let's hear one…. I could really go for a good joke right now.

MONROE

All right, it was this here white man and white lady coming from church. And the white woman was pretty of face…. Now it was this here slave coming from the fields picking cotton. He stopped to wipe the sweat from his face with this old rag he had. While he was wiping his face, he notices the white man and the white woman stepping onto their porch. He jumped up on the gate and sat down. He said, looking at the white lady in lust, "Damn, will I ever." The white man looked at him and said, "Nigga, you'll never." The slave said to him, "Where there's faith, there's hope." The white man said, "Yep, and where there's trees, there's ropes."

CLANCY

(Laughing) Damn, that was funny as a clown. Give me another one.

MONROE

You ever hear about how black folk got nappy hair?

CLANCY

Hell no! But lay it on me.

(Job rushes in with a business suit on. He has just come from downtown looking for a new job. But was stunned about what he saw)

JOB

(Breathing briskly) Man, It's your brother…. I went downtown… I come around by Main Street where they're constructing that new building, and there Sid was… Up on top of that big scaffold, flapping his arm like he was a bird.

(Clancy jumps up and goes into the kitchen to turn the lights off)

MONROE

Job, did he say anything?

(Clancy exits the kitchen with his keys in hand)

JOB

He just kept saying, "Fight him off you, Gray Dog…. I told you to go with the white-winged one…. You wanted to go with the black-winged one. I can't help you now. I'm looking for the white-winged one myself." Man, I tried to go up there and talk him down. But they wouldn't let me up there…. I told the police and them construction men I know him. They say they got to wait for some professional help to arrive…. Talking 'bout I might cause Sid to jump.

CLANCY
Monroe, come downtown with me and talk this man down.

(They exit the door. Lights go black)

ACT ONE
SCENE SIX

Three days after, lights come up in the restaurant. Debra and Patsy are at the table drinking a soda and taking a break. Sid is sitting at another table with a firm embrace on the seat of his chair.

DEBRA

Girl, that's what I said.

PATSY

I told Lisa he was no good. He left his wife for her…what makes her think he won't leave her for another woman? (Pause) Child, what is this world coming to…? Boy, that's a silly heifer.

DEBRA

Child, let me tell you what me and Clancy walked in on…. Three days ago… (Thinking) Was you here? Naw, you weren't here. Anyway, Nemo came by here to show me this new tattoo he got. It got these…

PATSY

Girl, will you hurry up 'fore Clancy come in here ranting and raving.

DEBRA

All right, you know his sister Janice?

PATSY
Yeah, what about her?

DEBRA
We come in here and Percy had her laid all out, like a lawn chair…. I mean tongue all down her throat.

(Sid sides his chair over to where they're sitting)

SID
(Staring them in the eye one at a time) I guess y'all didn't see me sitting over there? (Debra and Patsy, without speaking, race into the kitchen) Everybody wanna talk all over Sid, 'cause they ain't give over them wings yet. Just wait 'til they come with them white wings. (Looking at the kitchen door) I don't know why y'all running from Sid. He ain't gonna do you nothing…. Best watch out for that black winged ones… that's the ones y'all should run from. Don't know day or night from which they come…. See 'em everywhere. But if you're smart, you'll keep a running. (He takes his seat with him back to the table) See 'em at the hospital, going from room to room. Looking for the ones that are clinging to life… See 'em at nightclubs, just waiting for youngsters to get out of line. He on the passenger's side riding with the drunken driver. Just waiting for the crash. He on your bed-side telling your folks to go pull the plug, so he can nab the life out of you.

(Monroe and Clancy enter)

MONROE
(Sitting directly in front of Sid) How are you doing, Sid?

SID

(Holding onto his chair with a firm grasp while he rocks back and forth) Just making clear of them.

(Clancy sits at another table and lends an ear)

MONROE

Making clear of whom?

SID

The black-winged ones?

MONROE

Who are the black-winged ones? Where they come from? How many of them are there?

SID

They the falling ones…the ones that lost in battle. Sometimes one comes…sometimes many come. Depending on the case of the coming.

MONROE

What battle?

SID

The battle of the angels…. Shh. (He locks his feet behind the chair legs and closes his eyes. Talking confidently) Silence! Two are at hand.

MONROE

(Walks behind Sid) Where are they at? Point them out.

SID

I can't do that. They might grab hold of me.

MONROE

(Grabs a chair, sits beside Sid, and stretches his arms outward) I got my hands out. Ain't nothing grabbed hold of me. (Clancy tries to stop Monroe, but he brushes him off) Why they ain't grabbed ahold to me?

SID

(Opening his eyes and staring circuitously as if someone is encircling him) It ain't you they want.

(Debra and Patsy sluggishly enter the room)

MONROE

Who is it they want?

SID

Sid.

MONROE

Why do they want Sid? What has Sid done?

SID

Sid broke the spiritual barrier.

MONROE

How did Sid do that?

SID

He overlooked the physical eyes and saw with
his spiritual eyes.

MONROE

When Sid did that? Tell Monroe when Sid did that.

SID

When the white-winged one come for my daddy.

MONROE

Who is the white winged one?

SID

The white-winged one that come got my daddy…. The guardian since his birth.

MONROE

What happened when the white-winged one came and got your daddy?

SID

The day was getting dim. Daddy lay there on that bed with that cancer eating at his brain. Dr. Norwood just left the house 'cause Daddy was getting too stubborn…. Daddy calls me from the kitchen with his voice so low…. "Sid…" I come in there, and there the white-winged one was at the foot of my daddy's bed. I went right where it was and looked at it in the face…. The white-winged one's face was so bright it made my face gleam. I said to the white-winged one, "Who you be?" It just stared at me awhile and went and touched my daddy's forehead. The white-winged one touched my daddy's forehead, and another person come out my daddy with no clothes on. I looked at the face of that man, and it was my daddy. The white-winged one gave him something out of his mouth. Took my daddy by the hand,

and they floated up to the top of the room. I asked the white-winged one where he was taking my daddy. He said with his voice in my mind. "I'm taking him to his resting place. I will one day give you wings like I." Then they floated away.

MONROE
When he say he'll bring you them wings?

SID
Didn't say…. Just say he'd bring them. (He gets out of his chair and searches the room) But where they at. They ain't in here.

CLANCY
(He walks behind Sid and grabs his arm) Say, Sid, man, sit down and have a seat 'fore you hurt yourself.

SID
Let me go. Don't say nothing to me unless you can help me find them wings.

DEBRA
I know where your wings at…. I know just where they at.

CLANCY
Girl, what in the hell are you talking 'bout…? Don't start him up again!

(Debra looks at Monroe and winks her eye)

MONROE
Debra sure do know where they at…. The white-winged

one come by here yesterday and told her where they were…. Debra, would you be kind enough to tell Sid where they at?

(Clancy and Patsy looks at the conversation with an enigmatic look on their face. Sid rushes over to Debra to get his answer)

SID

(Exuberantly) They come, really…? You sure it wasn't them black-winged ones?

DEBRA

I'm sure it had white wings.

SID

That was the white winged one all right…? Where did he leave my wings?

DEBRA

I don't know the name of that hospital…. But Monroe know…. Hey, Monroe, what's the name of that hospital?

MONROE

I don't know the name of it. But I know where it is.

SID

Take Sid…. Sid wanna go where his daddy is…. Take Sid 'fore them black-winged ones try to take him again…. Take Sid to get his white wings!

MONROE

Clancy, should I take him?

CLANCY
(Sits down in mental anguish) Take him, Monroe…. Go ahead and take him.

(Monroe takes Sid by the hand and leads him towards the door. Sid stops at the door, walks back over to Debra, and takes her by the hand)

SID
You come go with Sid…since you know where his wings at.

(Clancy looks at Debra. Lights fall to black)

ACT ONE
SCENE SEVEN

The next day, lights come up on Clancy. He's sitting at the table figuring bills. Patsy has the restroom door open as she mops the floor.

PATSY
(Singing)
"Hallelujah anyhow,
Never, ever let old Satan get you down
When those trials come your way
Hold your head up high and say
Hallelujah anyhow."
(Humming)

CLANCY
Where you hear that song?

PATSY
Up home.

CLANCY
Where is up home for you?

PATSY
Vicksburg, Mississippi. I moved here with my foster parents.

CLANCY
What foster parents?

PATSY
You didn't know Earl and Ethel ain't my real mother and father?

CLANCY
Naw, I didn't know that.

PATSY
Yeah, they adopted me when I was six years old.

CLANCY
Hell, you look just like Ethel Mae.

PATSY
I know, 'cause she's my aunt.

CLANCY
Your aunt!

PATSY
Yeah, her and Earl adopted me when I was six.... Ethel is my mother's sister.... I had a sister that got adopted with me too. But she died, on my tenth birthday.

CLANCY
How she die?

PATSY
(Rolling the mop bucket into the kitchen) Snakebite...I can't really remember that much 'bout Ruby but her long hair and

how she died. (Pause) It's most likely 'cause I don't want to.

CLANCY
What brought y'all to Houston?

PATSY
(Taking a seat) Earl lost his job, so we moved down here with his mama and 'em. (Pause) Clancy, you believe Sid about them angels and all?

CLANCY
I don't know what to believe…. Janice with her gullible ass, chasing behind that nigga Percy.

PATSY
That's what Debra told me they got a lil thang going. I think that's nice. Janice done found her somebody.

CLANCY
Percy ain't no damn body…. Same as these other niggas. He's just after one thang.

PATSY
Percy ain't after that woman's body.

CLANCY
I ain't talking 'bout her body. I'm talking 'bout her money.

PATSY
Man, what you talking 'bout? Percy, them people got plenty money…. Got all them car washes and pool halls. Percy ain't after no money.

PATSY

(Grabs a rag and cleans off his table) Man, you getting yourself all worked up for nothing. Like I said, this lil seeing each other might blow off tomorrow…just give it time. (Pause) What time Debra getting here?

(Patsy exit)

CLANCY

She ain't coming today…. I gave her the day off.

PATSY

(Exiting the kitchen) You did what!

CLANCY

I gave her the day off.

PATSY

Look here, Clancy. I come here every day…always on time…and what I get? Not even, a dime raise. (Takes a seat at another table next to Clancy) Clancy, I know I don't have any kids, but I need a little money and a lil time off myself. These big legs get tired too. It's always (At a beat) Patsy, make the biscuits… Patsy, that order ready yet… Patsy, you write the menu yet… Well, Clancy, I'm sick of it! (Pause) I know you having problem with Sid and Janice and all. But, Clancy, I don't know how long I can take this abuse.

CLANCY

Patsy, I didn't know you felt that way. If it's time you need, you can take off today. I can take care of the place, and your new raise starts today. (He goes over and gives Patsy a friendly squeeze) Ah, I'm sorry. Big daddy didn't know. You tell Clancy what you need. He'll get it for you.

PATSY

(Slightly moving him out of her way) Move, man! 'Fore somebody come in here and think we got something going on.

CLANCY

We do have something going on.

PATSY

No, we don't either.

CLANCY

Look here, Patsy. Why don't we go catch a flick tonight? Not as no boyfriend and girlfriend, just two friends that ain't got nobody to love going to catch a late-night movie…. What you say?

PATSY

What I say is naw. Clancy, I ain't fixing to go out with you and have the whole Houston talking. You know how people talk. Say they saw you at the movies and add motel at the end of it. I ain't gonna give them people nothing to talk about.

CLANCY

Ah, woman, you just scared.

PATSY

Scared of what?

CLANCY

Scared that if you go out with me you might fall for me.

PATSY

Man, I couldn't fall for Billie D Williams right about now. Patsy done had all the loving she can stand for one lifetime. Back in the day, I had men on a waiting list. I done got too old for all that.

CLANCY

Women ain't nobody too old for love.

(Jabbo enters with a cage with a rooster in it. Patsy exits into the kitchen)

JABBO

Look out, Clancy, you seen that fool Percy?

CLANCY

That's the last fool I wanna see! What you looking for him for?

JABBO

That trick left our prize-fighting rooster out there in Peggy's yard. Wasn't leashed up or nothing. I asked Peggy what in the hell my rooster doing in her yard…. She sitting there on the porch eating a Jack Mack sandwich, spitting snuff juice everywhere. Talking 'bout (Mimics an old lady), "Baby, Percy, come by here last night in some fancy car. Let that rooster out and took off down the road." Took off down the road! It ain't not one road here in Houston. And that old hag talking 'bout, a dirt road. Man, I was so mad I grab this rooster by the neck, caged 'em, and left. Made me handle my baby all rough. Just wait 'til I catch up with that sucker.… (Kissing at the cage) Left my baby Wizzie in that old battle-ax yard.

CLANCY
I knew it! Patsy!

(Patsy rushes out of the kitchen)

PATSY
What?

CLANCY
Now he's riding her around in her own car.

PATSY
Ah, man, I don't wanna hear all that! (Goes back into the kitchen)

JABBO
Oh, he trying to push up on Janice. I hope he ain't forgot 'bout our big plans.

CLANCY
What big plans?

JABBO
My uncle got some land lil bit past Dallas. Say he'd let us have it for a few thousand.… Nice-looking land too. Easy to farm and everythang. Got a lil pond next to the house.… Man, it's nice looking. All I have to do now is come up with the money.

(The buzzer rings and Patsy exits the kitchen to take the order)

JABBO
What's going on, Patsy?

PATSY
(Enters the kitchen in a rush) Hi, Jab.

CLANCY
Well, let me get out of here and take Sid something to eat…. Patsy…you got Sid's food ready?

(Her voice is heard from the kitchen)

PATSY
I'm bringing it now! (She comes out of the kitchen and hands Clancy a plate of food) Tell Sid I said hello.

CLANCY
(Taking the food as he walks out the door) I'll call to check up on you. (Exits)

JABBO
Patsy give me a slice of that pecan pie.

PATSY
Ain't got no pecan pie…. Just sweet potato pie.

JABBO
Well, give me a slice of that.

(Job enters)

JOB
(Taking a seat at the table with Jabbo) What's going on, man?

(Patsy comes out of the kitchen and hands Jabbo a slice of pie)

Hi, Patsy. (Patsy looks at him, waves, and returns to the kitchen)

JABBO
You got it, man.

JOB
Where Clancy off to? He could hardly speak to me. He got in his car and took off. Where Debra at?

JABBO
I think she in there.

JOB
Hey, Debra…Debra!

PATSY
(Peeping in out the kitchen) Debra is off today…and keep your voice down. You gonna make my cake fall!

JOB
Sorry, Patsy…. She sounds like my mama, "Stop all that noise…. You gonna make my cake fall." Noise don't make cakes fall…. None baking people do.

JABBO
(Takes his plate and sits it behind the steam bar) What you looking for Debra for?

JOB

To thank her for the dress she bought Vanessa for her graduation.

JABBO

Vanessa sure did graduate this year…. She graduated with my cousin up there at Barbara Jordan. Man, time is ticking into the future.

JOB

Yeah, graduated at the wrong time too.

JABBO

Wrong time for what?

JOB

Man, you know they let me go last week, up there at Big Three…. Twenty-one years of fooling with that hard steel and they let me go without warning me.

JABBO

Yeah, man, I hear you…that's how they do you. Slave you for a couple of years and they take you out like dirty laundry. But me, I'm gonna control my own fate…I ain't fixing to be a slave on no damn job while the man can control my fate. Tell me when to take a break…. Tell Jab when to take a piss. Tell me when I can eat my lunch. Hell, what they think our race was fighting for?

JOB

My daddy told me to go ahead to college to be an engineer…. But me, I wanted to be all hot headed a get a good job and a fancy car. My daddy told me to get my book learning for a while and after that, I could be running my own business…. Told me that's why he named me Job. 'Cause it looked like I'd grow up to be a patience man…. But I turned out to be a stupid fool.

JABBO

Say, man, don't be so down on yourself. Maybe she'll get into one of them junior colleges…. Maybe even get in at Texas Southern University. They tuition ain't that high. Put her on that financial aid for a couple of years at the government's expense.

JOB

Done tried that already… They say I make too much money.

JABBO

You ain't making it now… You tell them that?

JOB

Jab, them people don't give a damn 'bout that. They only get involved when you stealing something or dealing drugs…. Other than that, they don't wanna have nothing to do with you. Just mess with theirs…. Just touch theirs. Then they wanna lock you up and melt the damn key. They can put you in jail, but they can't put you in college…. All these penitentiaries they build… Why not spend them taxes on building schools? A man works damn near every day of his life at the sweat of his brow and they take your tax money… and do whatever in the hell they wanna do with it. I say give some of it back so I can put my baby through college. (With anger) No, Mr. Smith…we are using this here money to give your brothers and sisters free room and board.

JABBO
(Grabbing Job at the shoulders) Say, Job, pull yourself together.

JOB
But Vanessa ain't got to worry 'bout it. Her daddy got him a
big three fifty-seven in the closet... that say she's going to
college one way or another!

(He slaps his hands on the table and walks out the door)

PATSY
(Entering the room) Jab, why you get that man started
'bout his job and all? Ain't no telling what's on Job's
mind.... Might come in here one day and shoot the whole
heap of us.

JABBO
Ah hell, Job ain't gonna do nobody nothing. He just mad
right now, he'll blow it off. (He goes over to use the payphone)

(Monroe enters pushing a stroller. Inside is his daughter, and
she is sound asleep)

MONROE
Hey, Patsy, where Clancy at?

PATSY
He just left out of here to take Sid some food up there at the
hospital. (Looking inside the stroller) She so precious....
Look just like Linda.

MONROE

Old Job still mad, huh…? (To Patsy) Go ahead. You can hold her.

PATSY

Naw, that's all right.

MONROE

Naw, go on and pick her up, she ain't gonna cry.

PATSY

Monroe, I told you it's all right.

MONROE

You scared to hold a lil baby?

PATSY

Damn, man! I'm on my cycle, okay?

JABBO

Hey! Y'all keep it down over there.

PATSY

Five minutes, Jab…. Monroe, what hospital you took Sid to?

MONROE

That new psychiatric hospital in the medical center. Took them eight hours to admit him. He sat there and talked to one of them nurses all night 'til he fell asleep. He was watching TV and everythang. Ain't give me no trouble. I thought he was gonna get down there and clown me and Debra. But he wasn't acting crazy or nothing…. Wasn't holding on to nothing. Sid even gave Debra a kiss and waved to her goodbye as we were leaving.

PATSY

That's good. He might be coming back to his senses.

(Jabbo slams the phone down)

JABBO

I told that fool not to go down there.

MONROE

Say, Jab man, what's up?

JABBO

The laws locked Jackmove up for gambling down there on Scott. All he had to do was just listen to me.

PATSY

Who told you?

JABBO

I was just talking to his cousin Boudreaux on the phone. Say Jack called him this morning and told him…. Damn, I'm glad I wasn't down there. That's all my parole officer would've needed to lock my ass up! Thank God for conscience.

PATSY

I told y'all that gambling stuff don't do nothing but lead to destruction. Look what it got June. Ain't no telling what they might try to give him.

JABBO

Ah hell, he won't be in there long…. Well, let me get out of here 'fore them laws come looking for me…. Talking 'bout I done did something. If y'all see Percy, tell him to get up with me. (He tickles Monroe's baby, grabs the rooster cage, and walks out the door)

PATSY
Can I get you something, Monroe?

MONROE
Naw, you don't worry 'bout us. Gone go ahead and do what you got to do… Just act like we ain't even here.

(The buzzer rings, and Patsy answers it)

PATSY
(At the pickup window) What you want, Nemo? Naw, Debra is off today…. All right, I'll tell her. (To Monroe) That was Debra's friend, Nemo…. Man come to the pickup window every day. What Debra done put on that fool?

MONROE
Probably done put some voodoo on him.

(Janice and Percy enter)

JANICE
(Leaning back in Percy's arms as she walks) Naw, you're the one who was afraid.

PATSY
So…where have you two lovebirds been?

(Percy takes a seat and Janise sits in his lap)

JANICE

To Astroworld…and Percy was terrified to ride everythang. Even the bumper cars…. I had to dupe him by giving him a kiss for every ride he got on.

PERCY

Ah, woman! I was just tricking you…. I was just trying to get me some sugar. I done been on every ride at that place…. But I was somewhat scared of that Texas Cyclone…. Now that was the ride I really earned my sugar. (Kisses her on the cheek)

PATSY

(Walking into the kitchen) I'm scared of y'all!

JANICE

(Leaning over toward the baby) She's so beautiful…. What's her name?

MONROE

Angel.

JANICE

That she is.

MONROE

You wanna hold her?

JANICE

Naw, that's okay.

MONROE

Don't tell me you on yours too.

JANICE

No, I'm not on my cycle!

PERCY

(At a friendly tone) Say, man! You better watch how you talk to my woman!

MONROE

Boy, what are you yapping about? Hell, I raised you and this girl.

PERCY

Baby get up for a minute, I got to use the restroom.

JANICE

Well, hurry up so we can go.

(Percy goes into the restroom and shuts the door. Moments later, Clancy enters with a frown on his face)

CLANCY

Janice, where in the hell have you been?

(Monroe takes the stroller off the safety and rolls it out the door)

JANICE

What you mean where I've been?

CLANCY

You know damn well what I mean…. Sid is losing his mind and you out there riding 'round like you Elizabeth Taylor or some damn body.

JANICE
Look here, Clancy…

(Percy walks out of the restroom zipping his pants up)

PERCY
(Trying to shake Clancy's hand) What you say, Clancy?

CLANCY
Man don't say a damn word to me!

PERCY
Damn, Clancy man, what I do to you?

CLANCY
Nigga just get out of my face!

(Janice walks over to stop the two from quarreling)

JANICE
(Pushing Percy in the chest) Baby just wait for me in the car.

(Percy walks out the door with a look of disappointment on his face. Patsy exits the kitchen)

PATSY
What's going on in here?

CLANCY
Patsy just go back in the kitchen. I have everything under control.

(Patsy reenters the kitchen)

JANICE

You have no right to talk to him like that.

CLANCY

What you mean talk to him like that… This here is my place. I run it how I wanna run it!

JANICE

You mad because I'm seeing Percy…. I'm a grown woman, thirty-five years of age, Clancy…I ain't that little girl you used to chase around the house…. I'm a woman!

CLANCY

Well, why don't you act like one! Your brother is damn near out of his mind…and you running 'round here with a nigga that ain't trying to do nothing but use you.

JANICE

All my life…all I ever did was listen to people telling me what's right for me…. Janice, get your book learning… Mama telling me what school to go to, Daddy talking about how hard he worked for me to get into medical school…. I love Daddy for what he has done for me. But why I have to owe him so long? You want me to take every cent I made and go toss it on his and mama's graves. Eighteen years of conveying death inside of me and it just kept accumulating up on me…one after the other. I love Gray Dog, Mama, and Daddy. But I have to keep living my life. Every guy I've met I ran them off because it was hard to just let go of my folks. I can't take stuff like this so well. I have had miscarriage after…miscarriage due to anxiety and sorrow…. I have to let go!

CLANCY

But what about Sid? The man thinking he see angels. Last week Monroe had to talk him down from jumping off a building and killing himself. He getting 'round here grabbing on anything next to him, thinking gravity gonna give out on him. Talking 'bout when Daddy was dying, an angel took Daddy away a promised him some wings…. He was in here yesterday searching the place talking 'bout he looking for his wings…. Monroe and Debra had to trick him into going to the hospital. (Pause) Look here, Janice, I'm not trying to run your life. But we are family…. You and me is all Sid got in this world. I understand you got your job and all, but Sid is our brother. We got to see him through.

JANICE

Clancy, what you want me to do?

CLANCY

Janice, I'm not asking you to babysit him. Just talk to him. Let him know your still here. He'll be happy to see your face.

JANICE

All right, when are we going to see him?

CLANCY

I think you should go see him yourself…. Give y'all a chance to get reunited.

JANICE

Well, I'll call you tonight and get the information…. Percy is out there waiting for me. (Walking towards the door) I'll give you a call tonight. (Exits)

(Clancy takes a seat at the table)

CLANCY
(Yelling) Patsy…! (Patsy peeks out of the kitchen) Go ahead and take off tomorrow.

(Lights go to black)

ACT ONE
SCENE EIGHT

The light comes up on Clancy as he takes an order at the pickup window. Jabbo has his face focused between a newspaper.

CLANCY
(Handing food out of the window) Okay, you had the beans, and chicken, with an extra cornbread muffin... That'll be $4.19... Come again now.... (To Jabbo) Jabbo, I hear Jackmove got locked up yesterday.

JABBO
Yeah, his mama and 'em went to make his bond this morning... He'll be down here soon.

CLANCY
(Sits at the table next to Jabbo) Sid is finally coming back to his senses. He trying to talk to me and everythang.... I took him some food yesterday; he stood at the door and gave me a hug. Nurse told me he keeps hugging everybody that comes up to him.... I wonder how long that gonna last.... Sometimes he talks to me, and at other times he just staring into space.

JABBO
Sid just going through a stage...can't get over all them deaths and thangs. It'll pass through.... (With joy) Damn, this a bad

car…. A nineteen eighty-eight Thunderbird…. Damn, if I wasn't trying to get that land, I'd be rolling in style…. Put me some music in there… Not that old, rap stuff them youngsters be listening to. I'm talking 'bout some Marvin Gaye. Put that "Ain't nothing like the real thing" in there. Man, I'll ride through Fifth Ward, and have them niggas sick…. (He gets out of his seat and starts to dance) You know Marvin Gaye be jamming…. Got that girl Tammi Terrell in the back, just backing up every word he say…. Damn, I'll have them niggas throwing up!

CLANCY

How much your uncle wants for that land and all?

JABBO

He said he'd let me have it for twenty-five hundred… But I know I can talk him down to twenty. He kind of a jighead. All I have to do is get him full of that Rock gut wine…. Might even get it for a thousand…. Damn, my uncle is stupid like that. Got all that land up in Lubbock, and he is living in that raggedy house in Leona. Clancy, you should see my uncle's house he lives in now. It looks like a closed funeral home. My uncle's wife is about three-hundred pounds and some change…. Damn, she big and ugly. All she does is sit on the garret, eat watermelon, and spit snuff… With them big crusty feet…. Woman's feet look like salt bacon. All you got to do is chop 'em off and put them in some greens. She beats my uncle too. You should see the back of my uncle's head. He got a big-ass lump at the back of it, where she done hit him in the head with a skillet, for not tying the feed bag on. (Pause) House is just nasty…. Don't make no sense for folks' house to be that nasty. I remember I went to his house one time to stay the night….

We walk through the door, and a big-ass rat was lying in the middle of the floor. I'm thinking he fixing to go and get a broom or something and hit him with it. My uncle went in the kitchen, turned on the light, came back in the living room, and kneeled to the rat. Talking 'bout, "Leroy... Leroy, get up and go get in the bed."

CLANCY

(Laughing) Damn you can lie... You know damn well that man ain't got a bed for no rat.

JABBO

I ain't lying, they just nasty like that.... Let them animals do damn well they please. Pigs right in the middle of the living room watching *The Price Is Right* and eating cereal with him. Tub looks like a swamp...he tells me it got some nice-size catfish in there too. (Pause) House smell like the farm is on the inside and the house is on the outside. That's where I got my baby Wizzie from. I come in the living room and this here big rooster sitting up on the couch. I was fixing to sit on the couch. My uncle said, "Boy, you best not sit there." I said, "Why?" I sat down on that couch, and that rooster went to work on me.... Cut up all my clothes...put a big plug in the back of my head. I looked at my uncle and said, "What in the world is wrong with that rooster?" My uncle said, "He don't like nobody on that there sofa." Told me that rooster is a prizefighting rooster. Say he done kill every rooster he done been against.... Say the rooster put a man in the hospital 'cause he tried to stop the fight.... Killed dogs and all. My uncle caged him up and gave 'em to me for my birthday. Damn rooster is so bull-headed, he won't even wake you up in the morning. Have me late for everything. One time I had to get up early to go see my parole officer and I was late. I got up looked at him...and the rooster was looking at me like, "Nigga, I'm a fighter, not an alarm clock!"

CLANCY

I remember Janice had an old chicken she loved so much. L.B. chopped his head off with his hunting knife.

JABBO

Damn, I wish I had known L.B. some. I always hear y'all talking 'bout him.

CLANCY

No, you don't either... Man, L.B. was the most devilish nigga you would ever wanna meet.

JABBO

Damn, I bet y'all had so fun coming up.... Had that big house in the country.

CLANCY

Yeah, but my daddy worked us hard...but he was fair.

JABBO

Hey, why y'all call L.B. Gray Dog, anyway?

CLANCY

'Cause my daddy bought Sid this dog for his birthday.

(Cadillac's horn is heard at the front door, and Jabbo goes to open it. Cadillac rolls his bike in. He is dressed in an old suit)

JABBO

(Closing the door behind Cadillac) Damn, old timer, where you coming from?

CADILLAC

(Puts his bike on the kickstand and takes a seat) Man, it's hot out yonder…. I went to Berta Re's funeral. Had 'bout ten limousines behind me…. I mean a heap of folk was there.

CLANCY

Damn! Berta Re's funeral sure was today…? David told me that the other day. It just slipped my mind. What you mean behind you?

CADILLAC

Man, I drove my bike to the gravesite… Wasn't nowhere but over there on Cleburne.

JABBO

Not Cleburne, on the end of Cullen. Don't tell me you rode your Cadillac all the way to the gravesite, in front of all them limousines.

CADILLAC

Hell yeah! I sang at her funeral.

JABBO

To tell the truth, I didn't know you could sing.

CADILLAC

There is a lot folk don't know 'bout me. They look at me and just see an old, dirty man riding a bike and think I'm some transient. Man, I done graduated from college and everything. Majored in Theatre Arts at Southern University.... I done been in more plays than a town of witches got spells.

JABBO

You might be able to blow a tune or two. But I know damn well you ain't been no actor.

CLANCY

Jab, you must don't know who you sitting by... All this time you been living in Third Ward you ain't know you been talking to a star.

JABBO

Man, I learn something new every day.

CADILLAC

You could learn a lot of things if you would ask people about themselves instead of assuming.

JABBO

How you end up falling?

CADILLAC

I started fooling with that drug stuff.

JABBO

Man, if God ever give me a big break like that, I'd never let anything mess it up. An actor on Broadway... Man, that's damn near every child's dream, to be on stage. Being on them big stages ever made you nervous?

CADILLAC

When I first hit the stage, hell yeah, I was scared.

(Jackmove bursts through the door crying with foolishness)

JACKMOVE
Man, y'all, come look at the sky…. The world coming to an end!

(They all run to the door in panicking silence)

CLANCY
(Noticing a false alarm, and hits Jackmove on the arm) Why in the hell you wanna play like that? That ain't nothing to be joking about. Somebody could have a damn heart attack.

CADILLAC
Man, I was 'bout to crap on myself.

JABBO
(Walking to use the restroom) Damn, man! Don't play with folk like that! Hell, I got to use the restroom now…. I think something done seeped out.

JACKMOVE
(Laughing) Damn, y'all some scary niggas… Scared of the world coming to an end…. The Bible says you gonna hear a big trumpet first…. That's how you know the world 'bout to end.

CADILLAC
Boy, you a silly man. Coming in here fooling with folk like that.

CLANCY
When you get out anyway?

JACKMOVE
My mama and her sister bond me out this morning.

CLANCY
They should have let you stay in there.

CLANCY
Say, Jackmove, don't come in here with that jive. You say anything that come to your mind. We was having a fine time until you came.

JACKMOVE
I'm just jiving around…. Where them girls at?

CLANCY
I gave both of them the day off.

JACKMOVE
Say what…? You gave somebody the day off. Business must be slow. (Taking a seat) That nigga Nemo Debra fools with… he got locked up with me. In the City Jail crying like a slave at a Klan rally…. Laws had to put them dogs on him…Me and him got into it over a game of dominos. They let him go early. (Goes over to the restroom to vex at Jabbo) Say, man, when you drop one, flush one. (To Clancy) Hey, Clancy, my aunt told me 'bout what happened to Sid. Is he okay?

CLANCY
Yeah, he's okay. Monroe and Debra had to trick him into going to the hospital. He's doing fine.

(Jabbo exits the restroom)

JABBO

I heard you won damn near two thousand dollars on that George Foreman fight last week. Hand some of it over.

JACKMOVE

Hell, I lost that money in the next three hours. I'm like that song that old frog-sounding dude sing, "I didn't say I was a millionaire. I said have spent more than a millionaire."

CLANCY

(Going into the kitchen) Boy, you mess up more money than NASA.

JABBO

What kind of bird don't fly…? Jailbird!

JACKMOVE

Say, man, y'all must haven't been having no dead ring cock-fights over there at Peggy's. I passed by there a couple of days ago, wasn't a soul near her yard. Got me scared. I thought the fuzz was out on the loose. (Pause) Where that rooster Wizzie at? He still making you money?

JABBO

Naw, he hasn't fought in a while. Folk scared to let their rooster at him. He ain't had a cockfight in 'bout a good two weeks…. Hell, right about now I'll let him fight some of these niggas running 'round here.

JACKMOVE

Where that boy Percy at? What have he been up to?

JABBO

Don't say nothing, but he fooling 'round with Clancy's sister Janice. Boy, that ran Clancy warm. Percy, driving her car and everythang. I bet she giving him money and everythang.

(Clancy exits the kitchen)

CLANCY

What y'all two knuckleheads gossiping 'bout?

JACKMOVE

We talking 'bout yo…

JABBO

(Cutting him off) We talking 'bout your prices…yeah, we talking 'bout your prices. How come everythang so high in here?

CLANCY

High hell! Much food I give you niggas for free, and y'all talking 'bout high.

JACKMOVE

Man, we just jiving 'round with you. Give me the most expensive dish on your menu…. I'll pay you tomorrow.

(Jackmove and Jabbo break out in laughter. Sid bursts through the door in a hospital robe)

SID

I done searched that whole hospital, and I still ain't found my wings.

(The lights go dark. End of Act One)

ACT TWO
SCENE ONE

A week later, lights come up on The Mudflats. Debra and Patsy are in the kitchen preparing food for the day. Sid sits at the table wearing temporary glasses from the optometrist. Clancy is at the chalkboard writing the day menu. "Meatloaf and two sides for $6.19."

DEBRA
(Peeping out of the kitchen) Clancy, we running out of sugar.

CLANCY
I'll go and get some later on.

SID
(Staring at Debra) Come here for a minute, sweetie.

CLANCY
Debra, get back in that kitchen…. Sid, she got work to do. She ain't got time for talking.

SID
Sid just trying to be kind…. Sid just speaking to her.

CLANCY
Well, you can chat with her later. She got work to do.

DEBRA

(Walking toward Sid) Sid just being nice. (Clancy exits into the kitchen) What can I get you, Sid?

SID

(Grabs her hand and gives it an aching grip) You can get Sid his wings!

DEBRA

(Pulling back from Sid in distress) Clancy… Clancy!

(Clancy and Patsy come to the aid of Debra)

CLANCY

What in the hell is going on in here? (Walks over to Sid) Sid, what in the hell you do to her? Debra, what he do?

DEBRA

I walked over to him to see what he wanted, he grabbed my hand and started squeezing it…talking 'bout get his wings for him.

CLANCY

Y'all go on back in the kitchen. Me and Sid need to have a talk. (Debra and Patsy walk back into the kitchen looking back at Clancy) Sid, what you do that for? That woman doesn't know nothing 'bout no damn wings…. She was just trying to get you some help.

SID

White wings…white wings!

CLANCY

White wings…black wings…pink wings, nothing. You keep

acting like that. I'm taking you back to that hospital. If you can't talk to people without grabbing them, I'm marching you right back down to that hospital. And you ain't coming back 'til you get your act together.

SID
(Taking off his glasses) Sid hungry! Bring Sid some food.

CLANCY
Well, Sid gonna have to wait…. Ain't nothing cooked yet. (Picks up his glasses and places them on his face) And put back on your glasses. That eye doctor said for you to keep them on for two days.

SID
(Taking them back off) Sid don't need no glasses. Sid's eyes is just fine… Sid need some food.

CLANCY
Sid can't eat what Sid can't see. (Placing the glasses back on Sid's face) And if Sid takes his glasses off again…Sid going back to that hospital.

SID
No, Sid ain't either! Somebody try and take Sid back to that hospital…. They gonna meet them black-winged ones.

CLANCY
Patsy bring this man a piece of pie or something, 'fore I lose my damn mind. (He sits at the table next to Sid. Patsy's arm reaches out of the kitchen. At the end of it is a slice of pie on a small dish. Clancy gets up and retrieves it) Here, and not another word.

(Sid takes the pie for eating and gobbles it down)

SID

(Slams the dish onto the table singing)
"I'll fly away, Oh Lordie, I'll fly away
When I die Hallelujah by and by
I'll fly away…"

CLANCY

Where did you hear that song from?

SID

Sid's grandma used to sing Sid that song…. Used to rock Sid to sleep on her terrace singing Sid that song. I never got the meaning of it all 'til Sid's Daddy. die. Sid's Daddy died, and that's when it come to him…. the meaning and all. 'Fore you fly away, you got to. get you some wings. Some get white wings… Some get. black wings. But the white-winged one promised me them. white ones…. But why do them black-winged ones keep. coming trying to give Sid them black ones? Sid ain't. dumb. Sid knows where them black wings take you…. They. take you straight to Hell, that where they take you…. I. told L.B. to go with the white-winged one…. He got there. first. But he wanted to go with the black-winged ones…. Why? 'Cause they black like him? Naw, 'cause two of them. run the white-winged one-off. (Sid goes over to the wall and talks to it as if he is talking to someone). Help him…take him with you, you got here first…. What. you mean you can't help him? You took my daddy. (Asking questions) You came to watch over him, not take him? Why did you watch over him and you knew he wasn't for you? (Patsy and Debra peek out of the kitchen, and Clancy waves to them to go back inside) Why do you keep talking to Sid in his mind? (With his hands on his ears) Say it out loud. Sid's mind hurts when you talk to him like that. God sends you to protect and what you do? You let them black-winged one's rule over you. Who is the saver of the Lord Jesus Christ or old Beelzebub the prince of darkness? You can wrestle with me all day, why you can't do the same with the black-winged ones? Well, look here. I ain't Jacob…I ain't gonna wrestle with you 'til daybreak for no damn blessing… and you ain't changing Sid's name. (Looking up) Come back here when Sid talking to you. Come back here and give Sid his wings! (Beats the wall in hostility)

(Clancy walks over and gives Sid a fond embrace. Patsy, glancing at the action, delivers food to the steam bar, then returns to the kitchen)

CLANCY
Sid, man, who were you talking to?

SID
The white-winged one.

CLANCY
(Sitting him back in his chair) Come on, man, have a seat 'fore you hurt yourself.

(Monroe enters. Sid put his head down and stares at the wall from the side)

MONROE
How is it going, Clancy? What's wrong with Sid?

CLANCY

He still carrying on 'bout that white-winged one and black-winged one's crap.

MONROE

Sid, you okay? (To Clancy) What you say to him?

CLANCY

I ain't said nothing to him.... He in here squeezing Debra's hand like he crazy. I got on him too. He calms down a bit...said he was hungry. I told him he got to wait, ain't nothing cooked. Then he started talking 'bout his wings. Patsy gave him a piece of pie... Next thing I know he over there at that wall...thinking he talking to an angel. You and Debra should have never got that man started with that wings stuff. Now I got to look out for Debra.... Monroe, y'all should have never taken Sid down to that hospital. I admit he was fine when he was at that hospital.... Hugging folk and everythang. Probably 'cause he thought his so-called wings was there.... He said he searched that whole hospital, and still ain't found his wings. I bet he didn't sleep none that entire week.... Up there, rambling through that whole hospital.... Y'all should've just let him talk that nonsense.

MONROE

I had to do something. You wanted me to just let him wreck your place.

CLANCY

Ah, man, Sid ain't doing nothing but acting.... Hell, I can handle him.

MONROE

Oh, was he acting when he was going to jump off that scaffold? Look, Clancy, I am not here to tell you how to take care of your brother...I'm just trying to help. Hell, that was the only way we could get him to that hospital. Shit, that was good thinking of Debra.... See, if you agree with Sid, you'll get more out of him. But if you don't tell him what he wants to hear, that'll just put him in a deeper state of mind.

CLANCY

I don't mind y'all trying to help Sid. But don't agree with him 'bout no damn wings.

(The buzzer rings and Patsy comes out to take the order)

MONROE

Hi, Patsy. (Patsy gives him a friendly wave and. a smile) Okay, man, I won't say anything else about some wings.

CLANCY

(Walks over to use the pay phone) Let me call and see when this man gonna come and fix this Jukebox.

PATSY

(From the window) Clancy, how much is the meatloaf special for today?

CLANCY

(Pointing at the chalkboard) It's on the board.

(Patsy takes the order)

MONROE

How is Ethel and Earl?

PATSY

(Entering the kitchen) They doing fine.

(Sid vigorously locks his feet around his chair and gawks franticly on every side of the room as if he's being detected. Monroe caresses Sid's shoulders, calming his fears)

CLANCY

(At the pay phone, waving to Monroe) Say, Monroe, let him alone.

MONROE

Monroe is here, Sid. He ain't gonna let nobody take you.

(Lights fade to black, and the music carries into the next scene)

ACT TWO
SCENE TWO

Lights come up later that day, and music is finally heard inside The Mudflats. Sid sits staring into space as Clancy wipes down the steam bar, singing tunes. Patsy has gone home for the day, and Debra is at the ordering window talking to her boyfriend.

DEBRA
Hey, Clancy, who is that singing?

CLANCY
Oh, that's Jimmy Reed.

DEBRA
(To her boyfriend at the window) That's Jimmy Reed... (To Clancy) What's the name of that song?

CLANCY
"Big Boss Man," and who is that at that window?

DEBRA
Oh, this Nemo.

CLANCY
Well, tell Nemo to order something or getaway for my window... I don't mean to be rude, but y'all letting my cold air

out…. Yeah, tell him to come on in…. I wanna see who it is that been letting my cool air out every day.

DEBRA

(To her boyfriend) He said come on in. (Pause) All right, then pick me up down there by Wolf's. (To Clancy) He said he left his car on…he got to run.

CLANCY

(Puts the rag down and takes a seat) What kind of car your fellow drive?

DEBRA

(Taking a seat next to Clancy, trying not to disturb Sid) A seventy-four Mercury…. It's a pretty big car…. Got that leopard interior.

CLANCY

Is it green…with a big antenna on the back?

DEBRA

Yeah…you know him?

CLANCY

I see him riding by my house sometimes…. Damn car be putting all that static on my TV.

DEBRA

(Laughing) That's my Nemo all right.

CLANCY

You really like that fellow, don't you?

DEBRA

Yes, I do. He makes me feel so rich inside.... He keeps me laughing all the time. Clancy, he got this lil face he makes, it is so funny. (Pause) People like to talk about him 'cause he used to deal drugs.... But he don't do that anymore.... You know how folks are, once a dope dealer, always a dope user. That's why we don't see each other that much.

CLANCY

Damn what people say! If I was to listen to what folk say, I wouldn't have a dime right now.

DEBRA

Clancy, why you ain't got no woman?

CLANCY

Ah hell, I got plenty women.... Just 'cause you don't see 'em don't mean I ain't got any. Hell, I got a lil hot mama go to Texas Southern University...but she's in grad school.

DEBRA

I been seeing that young woman bringing you things.... She drives a lil red Toyota.

CLANCY

Hey, stay out my business. (Sid gets up and walks into the restroom and leaves the door open. Clancy goes behind him and shuts it. Sid opens the door back up, and Clancy takes a seat) He just wants some attention.

DEBRA

(Entering the kitchen) Is Janice and Percy still seeing each other?

CLANCY

Don't even bring her and that clown up. Sid been here damn near two weeks and she ain't called or came by…. That's how she normally does. Sometimes I don't hear from her in a whole year at a time.

DEBRA

She'll be here directly.

(Clancy enters the kitchen, and Jackmove enters)

JACKMOVE

Jackmove, baby, who you thought it was?

DEBRA

June don't come in here with that fuss…. Sid is in there in the restroom, and Clancy is in the kitchen…he gonna run you off if you come in here with all that.

JACKMOVE

I ain't causing in no fuss (Notices the light from the jukebox) …Don't tell me this here Jukebox working. (Looks inside the jukebox) …Let me see what there is to play in this here old thang. (Reading) Wang Dang Doodle, Koko Taylor… Big Boss Man, Jimmy Reed. Ghetto Woman, B.B. King. Born Under a Bad Sign, Albert King… Bad, Bad Whiskey, Amos Milburn. Spoonful… Howlin Wolf.

(Clancy walks out of the kitchen)

CLANCY

Something you don't know a damn thang about.

JACKMOVE

Man, all you got is old cats in here.... How come you ain't got no Luther Vandross or Michael Jackson? Hell, I ain't digging them old cats.

(Debra enters the kitchen)

CLANCY

You can't dig them 'cause you ain't been through a damn thang. If you had been through all the things, I have been through, you would learn to understand the blues.

JACKMOVE

Clancy, you ain't that much older than me and still act like an old man. I'll put it like this. You like your music, and I'll like mine.

CLANCY

That ain't music y'all listening to...

JACKMOVE

I'm just gonna put it like this... You listen to your music, and I'll listen to mine.

CLANCY

If you wanna call it music.... Let me see what this man is doing. (Walks over and stands near the restroom door) Sid, you all right, man?

(Sid slams the restroom door shut)

JACKMOVE

Sid showed you... Hey, Clancy, let me hold something.

CLANCY

What, you wanna hold my hand? I knew you come in here for something. How much you wanna borrow?

JACKMOVE

Let me hold 'bout fifty dollars.

CLANCY

Fifty dollars! (Goes in his pocket to get the money) Here, man, and I want my money back in my pocket come this Friday.

JACKMOVE

Sure thang, man, you'll have it back by Friday.... You'll have it back with a profit.

CLANCY

I don't need the profit. Just have my fifty this coming Friday.

JACKMOVE

You'll have it back.

(Sid walks out of the restroom. At the front of his pants is a wet stain)

CLANCY

Lord, this man done locked himself in the restroom and still pissed on himself… (To Debra and she enters) Debra…keep an eye on the place. I got to take this man so he can change pants.

(Clancy takes Sid by the hand, walks out the door, and Sid shuffles behind him. Debra starts toward the kitchen but is stopped by Jackmove)

JACKMOVE
Your boyfriend Nemo was locked up with me.

DEBRA
So, what! What that got to do with me?

JACKMOVE
I was just letting you know...so you would know where he was last week.

DEBRA
I know already. You don't have to inform me.

JACKMOVE
Yeah, we was down there gambling and got caught... What you see in that nigga Nemo anyhow?

DEBRA
(Walking into the kitchen) Don't worry 'bout him. Worry 'bout yourself!

JACKMOVE
(Yelling) He ain't nothing but an old drug pusher.

DEBRA
(Exits the kitchen) Look here, June...whatever he does is me and his business.

JACKMOVE
Oh, you down with him?

DEBRA
Like four flat tires.... He don't sell drugs anymore, anyway.

That stuff is all in the past. I don't care if he did sell drugs now anyway. He treats me nice. He ain't like you sorry, trifling negros, like to use a woman up. So, what he's been in a little trouble in the past. So, what he went to jail last week. The point is he is still Nemo. He treats me nicely. So, go on talking about his past. But while you're doing so, take time out and think about your future. 'Cause your future is his past, but it gonna be ten times worst!

JACKMOVE

Me and that man ain't nothing alike. How you gonna put me in the same boat with that man?

DEBRA

Do not judge, or you too will be judged. For in the same way you judge others, you will be judged, and with the measure you use, it will be measured to you.

JACKMOVE

What in the hell is that supposed to mean?

DEBRA

Pick up a Bible and you'll see. (Enters the kitchen)

JACKMOVE

(Yelling) Woman, you crazy. Sitting up there letting that nigga trick you into believing he's something he is not. When he fractures your lil heart, you'll see! And don't come running to Jackmove when he dismisses you like school.... 'Cause I gave you your chance a long time ago.

DEBRA

Are you through?

(Jackmove walks over to her, grabs her bottom, and tries to kiss her)

JACKMOVE
I can make it back like it was when we were in high school.

DEBRA
(Pushing him away) Don't touch me! What has gotten into you? I never had a thing for you.

JACKMOVE
Sure, you did…you just can't remember

DEBRA
(Pointing at the door) June, will you please leave!

(Jackmove approaches Debra once more, and she exits into the kitchen. Jackmove exits the front door. The lights fade to black)

(Lights go to black)

ACT TWO,
SCENE THREE

Lights come up on the Monroe, Clancy, and Sid ten minutes after closing time. Monroe and Clancy are sitting back having a couple of beers. Sid sits alone looking tired and weary. It has been a long day.

CLANCY

(To Monroe) Watch this here. (He takes his beer over to Sid) Sid, you want a drink?

(Sid raises his fist at Clancy in a boxer style of fighting)

MONROE

Sid gonna knock you out with them big hands.

CLANCY

(Jumping circuitously as if he is in a boxing ring) Ah, hell, Sid ain't got nothing…. Ain't that right, Sid? Them old hands don't work no more.

(Sid gets up and forms a fighter's position. Clancy backs up jumping about, feigning to punch Sid)

MONROE

(Gets up to announce the fighters) In the blue corner… Weighing in at a hundred and seventy-six pounds… "Clancy the Roadkill… Cheapskate." And in the red corner… weighing in at hundred and something…" Spilt a Wig Sid." Touch gloves and come out fighting… (He leans over to Sid) Play fighting, Sid.

(Sid and Clancy dance around a bit. Clancy throws the first bogus blow)

CLANCY
I told you…you ain't nothing. Gorgeous George and 'em probably was scared of you down at that PABA boxing hall, but I ain't.

(Sid takes a weak blow at Clancy's face and hits the deck. Monroe rushes to Sid's aid. Clancy, in shock, backs up in dismay. Monroe helps Sid into the chair. Sid looks at Monroe as blood leaks from his mouth)

(Lights go to black)

ACT TWO
SCENE FOUR

A day later, lights come up on Debra and Patsy.

DEBRA

Clancy ain't called and let us know nothing…. Maybe, we should go down there to the hospital.

PATSY

Clancy said for us to watch the place…and that's, what we gonna do. We can't do nothing for Sid, we ain't no doctors… You just wanna go down there to be nosy.

DEBRA

I care about Sid!

PATSY

Debra, girl, I do too. But it's nothing we can do about it…. It's left up to the Almighty and the doctors.

JACKMOVE

What in the hell is wrong with y'all? Y'all look like them white folk 'bout to start slavery all over. (Goes over to the jukebox) I give y'all something to be sad about…. What y'all wanna hear, some B.B. King or Muddy Waters?

PATSY

June, we closed for today…don't start that thang up…. Don't put not a dime in it!

JACKMOVE

What in the hell you think Clancy got it fixed for? To let it sit up in here and look pretty? (Takes change out of his pocket)

PATSY

June, Sid is sick, have a lil respect.

JACKMOVE

I'll show some respect when he's dead…. But right now, I'm fixing to start digging me some blues.

(Debra races over and knocks the change out of Jackmove's hand)

DEBRA

Not in here you ain't!

JACKMOVE

(Raising his fist to Debra) GIRL, YOU BETTER SIT YOUR ASS DOWN SOMEWHERE! Who in the hell you think you fooling with?

PATSY

(Walking over) I wish you would lay a finger on her!

JACKMOVE

What, y'all gonna jump me? (Picks up a quarter from the floor, places it into the jukebox, and selects a track) I'll tear this whole damn joint up.

DEBRA

No, you won't either.

(The song comes on, and Jackmove hops on top of the jukebox)

JACKMOVE

Debra…what in the hell you gonna do? Go and get that nigga Nemo…. I want a piece of him anyway.

DEBRA

(Talking loudly over the music) You leave Nemo out of this.

PATSY

Girl don't worry about him…. The Lord will fix him.

JACKMOVE

Why you wanna put God in this? What, you an Evangelist now or something? I ain't scared of no damn God…. He wants some, he'll get his too.

PATSY

June Bradley, you're sick…you need some help!

JACKMOVE

Y'all the ones who need some help. (He takes out a half-pint of whiskey and takes a swig) Jackmove is just fine (At a beat) …Still got air in my lungs…blood running warm in my veins…a pocket full of money…and a half-pint of Wild Turkey…with just one sip gone from it.

PATSY

And that makes you a big man, huh…? Well, June, how you gonna feel when you wake up with a hangover…no more money in your pocket, and in jail? Or better yet, waking up in front of God your creator…telling you, "Depart from me I know you not." Then how you gonna feel?

JACKMOVE
I'm gonna feel just fine. (Take another taste of his whiskey and spits it onto the floor)

(Clancy walks in, goes over to the jukebox, and unplugs it)

CLANCY
Nigga…have you lost your damn mind! GET THE HELL OFF OF MY JUKEBOX 'FORE I BREAK YOUR DAMN NECK!

JACKMOVE
Come get me down!

CLANCY
I never thought it would come to this. (Clancy walks into the kitchen to get his gun)

PATSY
(Grabbing Jackmove's hand, trying to persuade him to leave) June, just leave…don't start nothing with Clancy, his brother is sick.

JACKMOVE
I don't give a damn about Sid…. He supposed to be sick. Hell, he's an old man…. Talking 'bout some damn angels…. Yeah, he done seen some angels all right…some angel dust.

CLANCY

(Coming out of the kitchen with his gun in his back pocket) June, I'm gonna tell you what I'm gonna do. I'm not gonna bother you…. Just hop up off my jukebox and go home and sleep it off…. I've been knowing your people for a long time…and goddamn it, I don't wanna have it come to this!

JACKMOVE

I'm gonna tell you what I'm gonna do…I'm gonna get out of here 'fore I hurt somebody.

CLANCY

Whatever, man, just get out of here.

JACKMOVE

(Flopping off the jukebox) Yeah, I'll leave. Hell, I ain't never got to come in this here joint. (Walking out the door) Debra, tell your man to watch his back. (Exits)

CLANCY

How in the hell June got in here?

PATSY

He just walks in…the door wasn't locked…. What doctors say is wrong with Sid?

CLANCY

Lung cancer…. They starting surgery on him in the morning. Say they gonna try and get it out 'fore it spreads.

DEBRA

I knew it was that when Monroe said he was coughing up blood.

CLANCY

(Taking a seat) Damn, I'm get'n 'round here horse playing with the man…and he got cancer the whole while…. I started to get him checked when y'all first tricked him to go down there…. They got my brother up there hooked up with all them machines and tubes in his nose. I started to take all that stuff off of him and wheel him out of there. That hospital ain't gonna do nothing with him but make him get sicker. I'm gonna first see how the surgery go…if it ain't nothing they can do for him, I'm just gonna bring him home with me.

PATSY

(Rubbing Clancy's shoulders, calming his fears) He gonna be all right… Your brother gonna make it through.

DEBRA

(Going to the pay phone) I'm gonna call Nemo to come and pick me up… Clancy, you gonna be okay?

CLANCY

I'll be fine, you just go ahead.

DEBRA

(Dialing the digits) Patsy, you need a ride home?

CLANCY

Debra, I'll take her. Just go on ahead and be careful.

(Debra talks to her boyfriend, then walks near the door)

DEBRA

Y'all take it easy…I'll see y'all tomorrow. (Exits)

CLANCY

One death after another. First my mother with breast cancer…my daddy with brain cancer…then L.B. with prostate cancer…. Now, Sid got lung cancer…. What kind of cancer God gonna give me?

PATSY

Clancy don't say that….

PATSY

Is Sid talking at all?

CLANCY

Ain't saying nothing…just squeezing Monroe's hand. Monroe's taking it harder than me, but he won't show it…. I guess he's doing it for my sake.

PATSY

Monroe still up there with Sid?

CLANCY

Yeah, he said he gonna stay up there until they through with the surgery and all. (Weeping a little). I just couldn't stay up there and see my brother like that, Patsy. All them tubes up in him…can't move a bit. Eyes wide open like he is expecting somebody to come in the room…. I'm telling you, Patsy, it don't look good.

PATSY

It just seems like that now. Just have faith.

CLANCY

(Goes into the kitchen and turns off the lights) Well, let's get

out of here. I got to get up early and go to that hospital to
see if there's hope.

PATSY
Don't have hope…have faith.

CLANCY
You sure are changing.

PATSY
Clancy, the only thing constant is change.

(They exit. Lights go to black)

ACT TWO
SCENE FIVE

Lights come up on Debra as she is taking an order at the pickup window. Patsy is sweeping the floor, putting forth effort to remain occupied. It is the day of Sid's operation and everyone is a bit apprehensive.

DEBRA

Patsy, do we have pecan pie?

PATSY

(Staying focused on sweeping) Naw, tell 'em we ain't got nothing but banana pudding…take it or leave it!

DEBRA

(To the person at the pickup window) We do not have any pecan pie, just banana pudding…. Well, fine then! (Leaving the window and takes a seat) The nerve of some people.

PATSY

That's why I didn't even take that order…. What. is taking Clancy and 'em so long? They, ain't called…. They ain't tell us what hospital the man in or nothing. That ain't like Clancy to just hide things from us like that.

DEBRA

Clancy just don't want us to get all worked up, that's all.

PATSY

It's a lil bit too late for that.

(Jabbo enters with his rooster in a cage)

JABBO

What is happening ladies?

DEBRA

(Walking behind the steam bar, with a look of depression on her face) Hi, Jabbo.

PATSY

Jabbo, why you bring that thang in here?

JABBO

Clancy let me bring Wizzie in here all the time.

PATSY

(Walking into the kitchen to put the broom up) Well, Clancy, ain't here now, so just get that thang out of here!

JABBO

Damn, what in the hell is wrong with Patsy?

DEBRA

She kind of upset about Sid.

JABBO

What's happened to Sid? He okay?

DEBRA

You ain't heard? Sid is in the hospital…. He got lung cancer.

Monroe and Clancy had him in here two days ago, just, play fighting with 'em. Monroe said Sid hit the floor and started coughing up blood and stuff.

JABBO

You are lying…. I got to get down to that hospital and see what's up… (Going to the door) What hospital is Sid in?

DEBRA

Clancy won't even tell nobody…don't nobody know but him and Monroe.

JABBO

That's sure is like Clancy's stubborn ass…won't even let his friends up there and see Sid. GODDAMN IT, CLANCY!

(Clancy walks through the door)

CLANCY

Goddamn it Clancy what?

JABBO

Why you ain't tell nobody 'bout Sid? 'Bout what hospital he's in and all?

CLANCY

He'll be here, you'll see him.

DEBRA

The doctors say he gonna be okay?

CLANCY

They say it ain't nothing they can do for him… Say in thirty-six hours, he will be brain-dead.

PATSY

(Exits the kitchen) Clancy, you got to take me up there.

CLANCY

(To Patsy) For what! It ain't gonna do no good. He can't talk to you.... Just stare at you without blinking.

PATSY

I just wanna see him!

CLANCY

No! I told you...you'd see him tomorrow.

PATSY

(Takes off her apron and flings it onto the floor) Well, I'll be here tomorrow when he gets here. (She runs out the door)

CLANCY

(Going to the door yelling) Hey, Patsy...Patsy! Goddamn it, you could have sworn that's her brother too.

JABBO

Can you blame her...? (Goes over to the payphone) Clancy, what is Monroe's phone number?

CLANCY

Monroe ain't at home... He is still up there at the hospital. He ain't been home in two days...I don't know why he got to stay up there.

JABBO

Still give me his number.

CLANCY

It's 673-4577…it ain't gonna do you no good. I told you he ain't there.

JABBO

Hello, Linda, this Jabbo…what hospital Monroe down at? St. Elizabeth's in Fifth Ward… Yates, what you mean Yates? Oh, on Yates Street… Thanks Linda, here. (Looks at Clancy as he leaves) Clancy, don't keep us out…. We got the right to see him too!

(The buzzer ring and Debra goes to answer it)

DEBRA

I got it!

CLANCY

Whoever that is, tell 'em we 'bout to closed for today.

DEBRA

But, Clancy, what about all this food?

CLANCY

Damn, this food! We'll preheat it tomorrow…Now help me shut down. I got some things I need to take care of. (Goes into the kitchen)

DEBRA

Oh, Clancy, this just Nemo… (To her boyfriend) Hi, baby… What dude? It had to be Jackmove…. What did he say to you? Nemo don't even worry about him, he ain't doing nothing but trying to sell a wolf ticket…. Okay, I'll be out there in a minute…. Clancy…that's my friend Nemo outside, he 'bout to run me to the house…. Is there anything you need me to do?

CLANCY
(Peeping out the kitchen) Naw, just be here on time tomorrow… 'Cause I'm gonna need you.

DEBRA
(She walks over and gives Clancy a peck on the cheek) Clancy, get you some sleep now.

CLANCY
What in the hell that was for?

DEBRA
(Leaving out the door) I don't know, just make sure you get you some rest. (Exits)

CLANCY
(Come out of the kitchen and takes a seat) Dear God, I know this is the first time we have ever talked… But can I have your attention, Lord…? I know I haven't been going to church on Sundays like I should…. But, Lord Jesus, I need you right now…more than ever. It's my brother, Lord…the last brother I have. Please lend him to me a little while longer. I'm not asking for years, just a couple of days. I just wanna be able to talk to him once more, to share a couple of smiles and kind words for a moment. Lord, he's my brother and I never got the chance to tell him I love him…. Now that I want to tell him, he probably can't even understand me…. Lord, all I ask for is a couple of days…. Will you grant a foolish man that? I'm not a promising man, you made me, and you know all about me…but I'll try to do right by you every

day you bless me to breathe on this here earth of yours. Now, Lord Jesus, go into that hospital and touch Sid's body…. Them doctors done give him up…. They say it ain't nothing they can do for him. Go in there and touch his body and show them you God all by yourself. If you don't heal him, Lord, I'm not gonna be mad at you…. I just have to take it as your will. (He gets up, turns the light out in the kitchen, and walks to the door)

(Lights go to black)

ACT TWO
SCENE SIX

The next day, lights come up on Cadillac as he parks his bike near the door. Patsy is placing leftover meat from the previous day into the steam bar.

CADILLAC

Hey, pretty lady, Clancy and them come here yet?

DEBRA

Naw, they ain't got here yet. Sit down and wait for 'em…. Can I get you anything, Cadillac?

CADILLAC

Naw, I'll be fine… Just waiting for them to arrive. You quit that other job downtown, huh?

DEBRA

Yeah, I had to let it go…. I was being late every day…. Clancy started griping and grumping 'bout me being late so much, I had to do it…. Cadillac, what's your whole name? I know your first name is Dempsey, but what is your last name?

CADILLAC

Cooper… Dempsey Cooper the third.

DEBRA

You miss being on them stages and all?

CADILLAC

Sometimes. (Pause) I could go back to acting if I wanted to. But it ain't in me no more. I had me an audition set up last year in New Haven, Connecticut…. A fellow I know by the name of Lloyd Richards wanted me to audition for this new play some fellow wrote by the name of August Wilson. Say the play called… "Your Turn Has Come and Gone" or something like that. I wasn't trying to hear him. It'll just be going back in time…. I done had my chance at stardom.

(Clancy enters. Monroe is behind him pushing Sid in a wheelchair that is attached to an air ventilator. Sid is motionless. He is dressed in a hospital robe and comfortable slippers. His face is very pale, but his eyes are showing he has the will to live)

CLANCY

Debra, make sure you don't spray no kind of aerosol cans in here…. It could seep in that air ventilator.

MONROE

Clancy turn the air down a lil.

(Clancy exits into the kitchen)

CADILLAC

(Staring at Sid) How they say he doing?

MONROE

(Scoots a chair close to Sid and takes a seat) I don't listen to them doctors…they'll say anything to keep you there so they can get more money. Hovering 'round your room trying to get every dime out of your pocket… "It's an extra charge for a TV." What in the hell Sid wanna watch TV for? Boy, I tell you, them hospitals are something else.

CLANCY
(Walking out of the kitchen) Say, Monroe, why don't you go on home and get you some rest.

MONROE
Hell, I'm all right. Can't sleep at home either. My baby girl Angel…

(Sid jumps a bit)

CLANCY
(Cutting Monroe off) Debra, Patsy ain't called, did she?

DEBRA
Naw, she hasn't called.

CADILLAC
Clancy, you hear from Janice?

CLANCY
Don't wanna hear from her either. Her brother is sick, and she get 'round here playing boyfriend and girlfriend with a fool she don't even know.

MONROE
She'll be by here some time or another.

CLANCY
Yeah, when they reading Sid's eulogy or probably when they carve his epithet on his tombstone.

MONROE

Say, Clancy, don't put your brother in the grave so fast…. Sid is still here with us.

CADILLAC

Yeah, Clancy man, you shouldn't say things like that.

CLANCY

Well, damn, it's the truth!

MONROE

If it is, it still ain't no words to be saying.

CLANCY

That there is my brother…damn it! I'll speak how I feel!

MONROE

(With forceful voice) Clancy, man, why you got to be so mule-headed? Ever since Sid got sick, you been pushing us away…. Won't let people even come up to the hospital to see Sid. Got mad 'cause I stayed up there at that hospital with him. Man, you need to quit acting like that!

CLANCY

Acting like what? You're the one always trying to play Sid's brother. Like I don't even count. Every time I try and talk to him you butt in…like what I say don't even count. That's why Sid never talked to me.

MONROE

Man, that's some childish stuff to be saying. Sitting up here talking 'bout the reason Sid won't talk to you is because I treat him nice. I can't help it 'cause I know how to treat people. That's nice and all you used to feed your brother every day. Just bringing your brother hot meals every day ain't gonna help cure his illness...but I guarantee if you would've added a couple of kind words with it, he'd be in a better state of mind.

CLANCY

Man, you speaking foolishness. Sid got cancer...words can't cure nobody from cancer.

MONROE

I know that, but at least it would've helped put him in his right mind, so he would've gone and got help.... Man, you just don't know how to go about things. Sid wasn't ready to leave that hospital yet.... The doctors would have at least given him something to ease his pain.... But naw, you wanted to be so bullheaded and took him out of there. Did-n't even wanna sign the release papers. Clancy, that wasn't professional at all.

CLANCY

Professional! My brother is sitting up here, with cancer eating at his lungs...and you talking 'bout professional.

(Sid jumps a bit)

MONROE

Clancy don't raise your voice like that in front of Sid.

CLANCY

Move... Don't tell me how to talk! Damn it, that's my brother...I talk how I wanna talk! Hell, I'll unplug that air ventilator if I want to… Call the funeral home and have a lil funeral by myself…. Might even cremate him.

DEBRA
Clancy don't talk like that in front of Sid.

MONROE
Clancy, you done gone mad.

CLANCY
If I done gone mad…what you doing still sitting in here?

MONROE
(Stares at Sid a bit and gets up to walk by the door) I don't have to stay in here and take this.

CLANCY
Bye!

(Monroe exits)

CADILLAC
Clancy, man, that's your friend. Y'all shouldn't talk to one another like that. Good friends don't treat each other that way.

CLANCY
Clancy done said what Clancy had to say. You don't like it; you can step too!

CADILLAC
(Walks over and takes his bike off of the kickstand) Clancy, shut down and go get you some rest.

CLANCY
Don't worry 'bout Clancy.

(Cadillac exits pushing his bike)

DEBRA
Clancy, what's wrong with you? It's like ever since Sid got sick, you been treating people like dirt. Monroe is your friend for God's sake…. We just put up with you, but Monroe really cares for you. You think he stayed up there at that hospital 'cause he loves Sid so much? He loves Sid true enough, but he has a different love for you…. Clancy, you're wrong for treating Monroe like that. (Exits into the kitchen)

(Clancy gets down to check Sid's air pressure)

CLANCY
(Looking up at Sid, as Sid stares off into space) Look at you… done started all this confusion. (Smiling) Half dead and still starting stuff. But your lil brother Clancy ain't mad at you… he ain't mad at you at all.

(Jackmove walks through the door. Debra peeks out of the kitchen, rolls her eyes at him, and goes back inside)

JACKMOVE
Clancy, I didn't come here for any trouble… I just come to pay you your money.

(He walks over to Clancy. Sid looks in the direction of Jackmove and shakes franticly)

CLANCY

Ain't no hard feelings. I knew you were drunk.

JACKMOVE

(Hands him the money, and Sid with all his strength tries to roll his wheelchair out of the way) What's wrong with Sid? Why he looking at me like that?

CLANCY

Naw, I turn up the air pressure…. Let me turn it down a bit. (Stoops to turn the gauge down)

SID

(With a low squeaky voice) The bla… the blac… the black…

CLANCY

You okay Sid…? Clancy, done turn it down.

JACKMOVE

Let me get out of here. I'll scream at you tomorrow.

CLANCY

Take it easy, June.

(As Jackmove leaves, Sid's fears slowly abandon him)

DEBRA

What did he want?

CLANCY

He just came by to pay me some money he owed me…. Damn, I hate I talked to Monroe like that…. Damn, I'm a fool!

DEBRA

Y'all will make up. Just call him up.

CLANCY

Naw, I'll wait a while…. Give him a chance to cool off.

DEBRA

Cool off! You were the one blowing your top.

CLANCY

I don't know what got into me. It's like something evil inside of me was making me say them awful things. Hell, Monroe ain't been nothing but good to me…. And I sat up here and mouthed him out like that. Damn, I'm an idiot!

DEBRA

You just got to watch the way you talk to people…. People ain't gonna take no any kind of talk from you. Damn, Clancy, you got two people to make up with, Monroe and Patsy.

CLANCY

What makes you think I got to make up with Patsy? She run out of here, I didn't.

DEBRA

See there! That's what I'm speaking on. You never wanna admit whenever you're wrong.

CLANCY

Ah, woman, go in the kitchen and mash me up some beans. I'm fixing to nurse my brother back to good health.

DEBRA

Not with no beans you ain't. I'll fix him up some of that chicken soup Patsy made the other day.

CLANCY

Make sure it's warm, not hot.… Bring some tea too.

(Cadillac rushes in pushing his bike and breathing rapidly)

CADILLAC

(Taking a seat, trying to catch his breath) Man, some dude just rolled by and shot June.

CLANCY

(In shock) When did this happen?

(Debra sits at the table and gives an ear)

CADILLAC

Just a while ago.… I come riding around the corner on Scott, across the street from that Express Market…and a dude driving a big green Mercury just drove behind June and shot him in the head six times. Got Channel 13 News out there and everythang. The police chasing that fellow in that green car right now.

(Debra gets up and runs out the door in tears. Lights go to black)

ACT TWO
SCENE SEVEN

The next day, lights come up on Clancy and Sid. Clancy is sitting at the table reading the newspaper. Sid is next to him clinging to dear life.

CLANCY

(Reading) After an extensive chase authority finally caught thirty-six-year-old Nathan Tippet.... Nathan is being charged for the slaying of thirty-two-year-old June Bradley... (Talking to himself) Damn, June man, I just spoke to you yesterday.

JABBO

(Entering) Reading bout Jackmove, huh? I just left his mother's house.... They sitting there on the porch blaming their self for getting June out of jail.... Damn, I'm gonna miss that fool. His mama and 'em told me to get in touch with Percy, see if he'd be one of the pallbearers with me. Hell, you can't depend on no Percy. He already done messed up my plans.... That's one pallbearer they can scratch off the list. June's mama talking 'bout she having his funeral at Clay & Clay Funeral Home over there in Fifth Ward.... Say June didn't have no church home. Damn, I know June ain't never step foot in no church...but hell, don't have his funeral way across town. She must don't know all the stunts Jackmove done pulled in Fifth Ward.

CLANCY

Damn Percy and my sister! They both ain't nothing but damn fools.

JABBO

They caught that boy Nemo… I know they beat him down.

CLANCY

I feel sorry for Debra…. I know they gonna give that fellow of her's life…might even get the death penalty.

JABBO

They might just give him life, but they ain't gonna give a nigga the death penalty for killing another nigga.

CLANCY

What in the hell he shot June for I wonder? Probably over some damn crap game…. That's why I tell y'all fellows to stay out that lady yard gambling.

JABBO

I don't go on Tuam Street no more… (Takes a seat next to Sid) How Sid doing, you tried feeding him?

CLANCY

Yeah, he had some soup yesterday…. Doctors don't know what in the hell they're talking about.

JABBO

Yesterday! Man, what you trying to do, starve him to death?

CLANCY

I'm gonna feed him in a minute.

DEBRA
(Walks in and heads for the kitchen, and Clancy stops her)
Hi, fellows.

CLANCY
You all right, baby girl?

DEBRA
Yeah, just let me go in the kitchen and pull myself together.
(Enters the kitchen)

(Sid shakes his legs and tries rolling to the restroom)

JABBO
What's wrong with Sid? Why he shaking like that?

CLANCY
He has to use the restroom…. The doctor talking 'bout he got thirty-six hour to live…. Hell, he might outlive all of us. (Wheels Sid into the restroom)

(Debra enters wiping off tears from her cheek)

JABBO
Debra…look here, I'm sorry I talked about Nemo's car and all. I was just jiving with you. Hell, I…

DEBRA
I know… (Smiling a little) You tried to buy it before he got it painted…I ain't mad at you. I'm just missing Nemo right now, all that falling in love for nothing.

JABBO

Debra, girl, you got plenty of time for love…another fellow will come along.

DEBRA

Yeah, then he'll be gone too…I just ain't got no luck with men.

JABBO

Naw, the men just ain't know how lucky they were. Look at you.

DEBRA

(Hugging Jabbo) Thanks for caring about me and my feeling so much.

(Clancy rolls Sid out of the restroom)

CLANCY

(Smiling) Look at you… Your man ain't even gone before a judge and you cheating on him already.

DEBRA

(Wiping away her tears of joy) Shut up, Clancy. (Pause) Did you call up Monroe like we talked about?

CLANCY

Yeah, I called him, but Linda said he wasn't there.

DEBRA

Well, keep calling…you just trying to wait 'til he come see you.

JABBO

What you done did to Monroe?

CLANCY

We fell out over some words.

JABBO

Clancy, you good people and all…but you got to watch how you talk to people.

CLANCY

I'm working at it.

(Monroe walks in. He and Clancy lock eyes. Debra and Jabbo look at them for a moment and walk into the kitchen)

MONROE

I got your call. I was at home…. I just told Linda to say I wasn't there.

CLANCY

Look, man, I didn't mean any of that junk I said…. I was just being bullheaded like you said. The fact is, I was getting jealous 'cause you were giving Sid all the attention…. Man, me and you ain't never fell out before.

MONROE

I was the one being bull headed. Wouldn't even let you take care of your own brother…. Hell, I damn near got kicked out my own house…you ain't the only one I got to make up with. (Kneeling down to Sid) Sid, we sorry fighting over you like this…. Man, you just don't know how much you mean to us.

CLANCY

(Touching Monroe on the shoulder) You just don't know how

much you mean to me. (Monroe gives Clancy a close embrace) Thanks for being by my side.

(Debra and Jabbo enter)

DEBRA

That's what I'm talking 'bout. Get it together, y'all better than that.

MONROE

(To Debra) I'm sorry 'bout what happened to your boyfriend and all. Damn, I could feel something bad was gonna happen to lil June. Shock the mess out of me when I saw it on the news.

CLANCY

One minute you here…the next minute, you gone.

(Job steps through the door sporting a new suit)

MONROE

Damn, man, you sharp…. Where in the hell you off to?

JOB

Done got me a new job…. Y'all, looking at the new general foreman of Brown and Root. Got the job yesterday…good benefits and all. Got my own company car and everythang… a Lincoln town car, brand new…. Come take a look.

(They all march outside to see Job's company automobile. When they exit, Sid leans forward in his chair and coughs abundantly. He takes one deep breath and falls back in his chair. Sid looks forward and stares off as if someone has arrived to take him off on an extensive

journey. He smiles awhile and declines over and dies. Everyone enters
the restaurant in laughter. They all stare at the sight of Sid's death
and calmly crowd him)

JABBO
Y'all give him some room.

CLANCY
(Staring at his brother in awe) Jab, ain't no need… he's gone.

MONROE
(Slowly walking to the payphone) Clancy, I'll call and make
the funeral arrangements.

JOB
I'm sorry, Clancy.

CLANCY
Job, he was fixing to leave us anyway.

JOB
Well, I must be getting on to work. Clancy, I'll come by and
get all the information from you. (Exits)

CLANCY
(Staring at Sid in tears) Debra, look in there in the kitchen
and get that white cover off the table so I can put it over him.

MONROE
(Hanging the phone up) I talked to Mr. Mitchell…. He said
just give Sid's life insurance policy to the undertakers when
they arrive.

(Debra exits the kitchen with the sheet, and Clancy takes it and places it on Sid)

CLANCY

(Reaches down to turn off the air ventilator) Monroe, who did you call, Frazier Mitchell Funeral Home?

MONROE

Yeah, he is sending the undertakers now…. I'll meet you up at Mitchell's. (Hugs Clancy and exits)

JABBO

Clancy, is there anything you need me to do?

CLANCY

Just give me a little time alone.

(Jabbo shakes Clancy's hand and walks out the door)

DEBRA

(Staring at Sid and Clancy in sorrow) Clancy, I'll be in the kitchen if you need me.

CLANCY

Naw, Debra, go on home. I'm gonna go ahead and close up early…. The undertakers are on their way. Just put that close sign in the window. (Debra puts the sign into the window, kisses Clancy on the cheek, and exits. As she is leaving, Janice enters. She is worn after a lengthy day at work, and she's still dressed in her doctor's uniform. Janice notices Clancy sitting alone, next to someone under a sheet)

JANICE

(Walking over to Clancy in tears) Clancy…is… hat…Sid…?

CLANCY

(Sarcastically, in tears) It sure is.

JANICE

(Shakes, reaching her hands out to touch Sid) Can I see him?

CLANCY

Now, after all this time, you wanna see him…? After his blood no longer run warm in his veins, you wanna see him? Do you know how much pain you caused me? Sid lying in the hospital ending his life with cancer…and you somewhere playing doctor. You never did care about anybody in the family. Nobody but Mama… When Mama died, you blocked us out of your life like we was nothing…. The only reason you talked to Daddy 'cause he was paying your tuition.

JANICE

That's not true! I loved my whole family.

CLANCY

You liked us…. Like and love is two different feelings. (Reaching into his pocket and pulls out a roll of money) See this here? I like having money! (Tosses it to the floor and goes over to the jukebox) I like good music! (Walks over and raises the sheet from Sid) See this man right here…I loved that man… You can't love nobody you don't know. You didn't think to go see Sid…. I bet every time you saw him downtown, you passed him up like he was just another bum on the streets…. While I'm going down there, clothing him…chasing him down to feed him…you didn't call to see how we were doing… Hell, the both of us could have been dead… hell, you wouldn't have known.

JANICE

Clancy, I do love y'all… I was just so wrapped up in my career.

CLANCY

Go on, have your career. You a grown woman. I wish you and you man Percy a good future. May y'all life be the opposite of mine…. I wish nobody the kind of life I have. Now…if you would excuse me, I have a funerary service to prepare for.

JANICE

Can I help with the funeral expenses?

CLANCY

(Covering Sid's face, with the sheet) No! 'Cause you ain't invited to the funeral nor the gravesite… Now would you please leave us.

(Janice bursts out in tears as she runs out the door. Lights go dark as Clancy stares at Sid)

ACT TWO
SCENE EIGHT

Eight days later, lights come up in the restaurant. Everyone has just come back from the burial site of Sid. Patsy and Debra are behind the steam bar, preparing food, while the men sit at the table talking among each other. Clancy is in the kitchen fixing drinks.

JABBO

Cadillac was on the other end. He damn near dropped the casket.

(The fellows laugh)

CADILLAC

Hell, that wasn't me. That was Monroe… talking 'bout, "Jab, it's slipping…nigga, get it 'round on that side." Had his own wife laughing at him… Monroe, how come Linda ain't coming to the dinner?

MONROE

She coming…. She went to drop the kids off at her mother's house.

PATSY

(From the steam bar) Dempsey that sure was a lovely song you sang at the funeral…brought tears to my eyes.

CADILLAC

I sang the same song at June's funeral yesterday.

JABBO

Damn, old timer, we were there. (Pause) Yeah, Cadillac, you sung that song…but that choir sounded terrible. Trying to sing "Feel Like Going On." Made me feel like going home.

CLANCY

(Comes out of the kitchen and places their drinks next to them) Jab, you were up there singing along with them.

JABBO

Hell! I was trying to help them out.

(Patsy takes a tray of meat and sits it in the middle of the table and takes a seat)

MONROE

Bring it on, ladies.

(Debra brings the rest of the food and takes a seat)

CLANCY

Patsy, will you say grace for us?

JABBO

Grace!

CLANCY

I knew somebody was gonna say that.

PATSY
(Patsy stands up at the table to say grace) Will you all bow your heads in prayer? (Pause) Lord, we thank you for such a glorious evening. Lord, as we assemble here to eat…we give you thanks. Not for just this food…for all your many blessings. Lord, we're so happy today, 'cause we know Sid is in your care, Lord…. God, we realize that we all must come this way. You lend us a spirit…and someday we will have to return it…. Most of all, we thank you for the closeness between us. We also understand that you are the ultimate friend. (Janice and Percy enter and stand near the door) Now, Lord Jesus, let this food nourish our minds, bodies, and souls so that we may grow stronger in your name… Amen.

(Heads come up. Clancy gets out of his seat and notices Janice and Percy standing at the door)

JANICE
(In tears) Sorry to intrude, Clancy, but I had to see you.

CLANCY
(Clancy goes over to give Janice a tight squeeze and a kiss) Don't cry, baby girl. Time out for crying. It's time to start living. (Wiping away her tears) I saw you sitting on the back pew. I was trying to get your attention to come up there with me.

JANICE
(Smiling) I thought you were telling me to leave.

CLANCY
(Shaking Percy's hand) Thanks for coming, man.

PERCY

Anytime, Clancy.

CLANCY

(Walking them over to the table) Jab.

JABBO

What!

CLANCY

Nigga get up and let my sister sit down.

(Jabbo gets out of his seat and gives Percy a handshake. Patsy pulls out another chair for Jabbo)

PATSY

Good, we back family again!

MONROE

Clancy, did I ever tell you the one my daddy said about the guy that refused to go to the army?

CLANCY

Naw, lay it on me.

(Debra gets up and walks into the kitchen)

MONROE

Well, it was this here fellow fresh out of high school. He was just sitting at home, no job, no chores, or nothing. So, the mailman came and dropped the mail. He got the mail and opened it. It said that he has just been selected for the US Army…. Now, he was getting these letters 'bout a week at a time, and kept ripping them up. So, the army sent an army officer to come and get him. The officer knocked on the door, and there stood a tall black man. The officer said, "Sir, you have been just selected for the US Army." The fellow said, "You can't put me in the army, one of my legs shorter than the other." And raised his pant leg. The army recruiter looked at him and said, "Don't worry about it. Where you going, the ground ain't leveled noway."

(They all laugh. Debra returns holding a white sheet. Stuck at the end of the sheet are small white feathers)

DEBRA
Clancy…who put these feathers on this sheet?

(They all stare at the sheet. Moments later, the light goes black. End of scene. End of Play)

Art Illustration/Jordan D'Neal Stewart is a brilliant 16-year-old honor student and a Blessed young lady of so many talents. With performance in her blood, she first hit the stage at just 7 years old in Houston's *Ensemble Theatre's, Young Performance.* **Jordan D'Neal Stewart** is a brilliant 16-year- old honor student, and a Blessed young lady with so many talents, that her parents can barely keep up. With performance in her blood. She first hit the stage at just 7 years old in the *Ensemble Theatre's, Young Performance Theatre Training Program.* In her first two-stage performances, she stunned audiences with her amazing, huge voice in the musicals *"Princess"* by Judy Wicklund and *"The Adventures of Little Red"* by Broderick Jones's singing the songs *"Shy"* from the musical *"Princess and the Pea"* and *"And I Am Telling You"* from the renowned *"Dream Girls* "musical. Her family realized she had a true innate talent for performance and continued her training in Broderick Jones's **"The Talented Tenth" Summer Intensive Performance Program** where she flourished immensely in learning the business of performance. Her latest work consists of voice-over work for **Sesame Street** and acting in the **"Fifth Ward" series** on **Amazon Prime** and UMC.TV, with Jordan in the role of Latasha. Jordan has always had a love of music and writes and produces her original songs, composes amazing symphonic music, and is a self-taught musician on several instruments such as the ukulele, acoustic guitar, clarinet, electric guitar, piccolo, and finally, has been awarded the solo flute piece in her upcoming UIL competition for her High School Band. With all of that to keep her busy, she has still managed to perfect, yet another craft and this one may just be her fav of them all! **ART**, drawing, and animation have taken her dreams to new heights. She is now **writing** and **illustrating** several of her graphic novels and we can't wait! In the meantime, she pauses to create beautiful artwork for her clients, creating logos, birthday cards, beautifully unique hand-drawn **ABC sound cards for kids** sold on ebony-gifts.com, and book covers. Special thanks to Donyail Linsey for being her very first book cover client for his new play **"Spirits of the Mississippi River"** now available in every bookstore.